GENDER ISSUES IN
INTERNATIONAL EDUCATION

REFERENCE BOOKS IN INTERNATIONAL EDUCATION
VOLUME 43
GARLAND REFERENCE LIBRARY OF SOCIAL SCIENCE
VOLUME 1162

REFERENCE BOOKS IN INTERNATIONAL EDUCATION

EDWARD R. BEAUCHAMP, *Series Editor*

EDUCATION IN THE PEOPLE'S
REPUBLIC OF CHINA,
PAST AND PRESENT
An Annotated Bibliography
by Franklin Parker
and Betty June Parker

EDUCATION IN SOUTH ASIA
A Select Annotated Bibliography
by Philip G. Altbach, Denzil
Saldanha, and Jeanne Weiler

TEXTBOOKS IN THE THIRD WORLD
Policy, Content, and Context
by Philip G. Altbach
and Gail P. Kelly

TEACHERS AND TEACHING
IN THE DEVELOPING WORLD
by Val D. Rust and Per Dalin

RUSSIAN AND SOVIET EDUCATION,
1731–1989
*A Multilingual Annotated
Bibliography*
by William W. Brickman
and John T. Zepper

EDUCATION IN THE ARAB GULF
STATES AND THE ARAB WORLD
An Annotated Bibliographic Guide
by Nagat El-Sanabary

EDUCATION IN ENGLAND
AND WALES
An Annotated Bibliography
by Franklin Parker
and Betty June Parker

UNDERSTANDING EDUCATIONAL
REFORM IN GLOBAL CONTEXT
Economy, Ideology, and the State
edited by Mark B. Ginsburg

EDUCATION AND SOCIAL CHANGE
IN KOREA
by Don Adams
and Esther E. Gottlieb

THREE DECADES OF PEACE
EDUCATION AROUND THE WORLD
An Anthology
edited by Robin J. Burns
and Robert Aspeslagh

EDUCATION AND DISABILITY
IN CROSS-CULTURAL PERSPECTIVE
edited by Susan J. Peters

RUSSIAN EDUCATION
Tradition and Transition
by Brian Holmes, Gerald H. Read,
and Natalya Voskresenskaya

LEARNING TO TEACH
IN TWO CULTURES
Japan and the United States
by Nobuo K. Shimahara
and Akira Sakai

EDUCATING IMMIGRANT CHILDREN
*Schools and Language Minorities
in Twelve Nations*
by Charles L. Glenn
with Ester J. de Jong

TEACHER EDUCATION IN
INDUSTRIALIZED NATIONS
Issues in Changing Social Contexts
edited by Nobuo K. Shimahara
and Ivan Z. Holowinsky

EDUCATION AND DEVELOPMENT
IN EAST ASIA
edited by Paul Morris
and Anthony Sweeting

THE UNIFICATION OF
GERMAN EDUCATION
by Val D. Rust and Diane Rust

WOMEN, EDUCATION, AND
DEVELOPMENT IN ASIA
Cross-National Perspectives
edited by Grace C.L. Mak

GENDER ISSUES IN INTERNATIONAL EDUCATION
BEYOND POLICY AND PRACTICE

EDITED BY
SHEENA ERSKINE AND MAGGIE WILSON

Routledge
Taylor & Francis Group

LONDON AND NEW YORK

First published 1999 by
Falmer Press

2 Park Square, Milton Park, Abingdon, Oxon OX14 4RN
711 Third Avenue, New York, NY 10017, USA

Routledge is an imprint of the Taylor & Francis Group, an informa business

First issued in paperback 2016

Library of Congress Cataloging-in-Publication Data
Gender issues in international education : beyond policy and practice
    / edited by Sheena Erskine and Maggie Wilson.
            p.   cm. -- (Garland reference library of social science ; v.
    1162. Reference books in international education ; v. 43)
        Includes bibliographical references and index.
        1. Educational equalization--Cross-cultural studies.   2. Women-
    -Education--Cross cultural studies.   3. Sex discrimination in
    education--Cross-cultural studies.   4. Sex differences in education-
    -Cross-cultural studies.   I. Erskine, Sheena.   II. Wilson, Maggie.
    III. Series: Garland reference library of social science : v. 1162.
    IV. Series: Garland reference library of social science.   Reference
    books in international education ; vol. 43.
    LC213.G45   1998
    379.2'6--dc21   98-8644
                                                                                              CIP

ISBN 13: 978-0-8153-2861-2 (hbk)
ISBN 13: 978-1-138-97498-2 (pbk)

Contents

Series Editor's Foreword

This series of scholarly works in comparative and international education has grown well beyond the initial conception of a collection of reference books. Although retaining its original purpose of providing a resource to scholars, students, and a variety of other professionals who need to understand the role played by education in various societies or world regions, it also strives to provide accurate, relevant, and up-to-date information on a wide variety of selected educational issues, problems, and experiments within an international context.

Contributors to this series are well-known scholars who have devoted their professional lives to the study of their specializations. Without exception these men and women possess an intimate understanding of the subject of their research and writing. Without exception they have studied their subject not only in dusty archives, but have lived and traveled widely in their quest for knowledge. In short, they are "experts" in the best sense of that often overused word.

In our increasingly interdependent world, it is now widely understood that it is a matter of military, economic, and environmental survival that we understand better not only what makes other societies tick, but also how others, be they Japanese, Hungarian, South African, or Chilean, attempt to solve the same kinds of educational problems that we face in North America. As the late George Z. F. Bereday wrote more than three decades ago: "[E]ducation is a mirror held against the face of a people. Nations may put on blustering shows of strength to conceal public weakness, erect grand façades to conceal shabby backyards, and profess peace while secretly arming for conquest, but how they take care of their children tells unerringly who they are" (Comparative Methods in Education, New York: Holt, Rinehart and Winston, 1964, p. 5).

Perhaps equally important, however, is the valuable perspective that studying another education system (or its problems) provides us in understanding our own system (or its problems). When we step beyond our own limited experience and our commonly held assumptions about schools and learning in order to look back at our system in contrast to another, we see it in a very different light. To learn, for example, how China or Belgium handles the education of a multilingual society; how the French provide for the funding of public education; or how the Japanese control access to their universities enables us to better understand that there are reasonable alternatives to our own familiar way of doing things. Not that we can borrow directly from other societies. Indeed, educational arrangements are inevitably a reflection of deeply embedded political, economic, and cultural factors that are unique to a particular society. But a conscious recognition that there are other ways of doing things can serve to open our minds and provoke our imaginations in ways that can result in new experiments or approaches that we may not have otherwise considered.

Since this series is intended to be a useful research tool, the editor and contributors welcome suggestions for future volumes, as well as ways in which this series can be improved.

Edward R. Beauchamp
University of Hawaii

Foreword

The impetus for this volume followed the 1992 meeting of the World Congress of Comparative Education Societies, which provides an opportunity at three-year intervals for the presentation of research, discussion and debate. The Commission on Women and Girls brings together researchers to discuss current issues in the area of gender and education. Inspired to begin the project and pursue gender issues on an international scale, we are pleased to present this examination of gender issues in international education. The focus on equal opportunity policies and practice come at a time when many countries own a strategy and state a plan to promote the interests of women and girls in education. The need for such a volume is clear to us. In 1989 the United Nations reported that women made up two-thirds of the world's illiterate; worldwide in industry women still earned only two-thirds of men's pay for doing the same jobs; women, who comprised more than half of the world's population at that time, were hardly represented in the world's parliaments; and for every one hundred ministerial-level decision-makers there were only four women. Women were referred to as "the silent majority."

Since then the United Nations has gone on to encourage action on behalf of women. A Global Strategy — initiated in Beijing in 1995 by the United Nations Congress on Women, and supported by a Forum of Non-Governmental Organisations — was born and this placed a great responsibility upon education to effect an improvement in the lot of women generally. How can education help, especially when gender issues remain largely the issues of equality and social justice? What might girls and women expect from their education systems worldwide? In an attempt to answer these questions, we bring together a detailed examination of stated positions of national policy on equal opportunity with contemporary research evidence to reveal the congruence or lack of it between policy and practice.

Preparation of this volume has been both stimulating and enjoyable, thanks to the dedication and professionalism of the contributors, always so willing and able to meet the inevitable demands such a project makes.

Production of the book has brought reward to its editors, both in professional collaboration and in friendship. We are grateful for the forbearance of contributors, all with demanding schedules, who were willing to attend to detail. This was of immense help in smoothing the way to publication.

Our thanks go to Professor Edward Beauchamp, the Garland series editor, and to Marie Ellen Larcada, formerly of Garland Publishing, for their confidence in the project from start to finish. To our families a special word of thanks for their support during a time of professional and personal change.

Sheena Erskine and Maggie Wilson

Introduction

Sheena Erskine and Maggie Wilson

The United Nations Convention on the "Elimination of All Forms of Discrimination against Women" became an international treaty on September 3, 1981. All countries whose representatives signed the treaty are committed to take all appropriate measures to ensure the full development and advancement of women, for the purpose of guaranteeing them the exercise and enjoyment of human rights and fundamental freedoms on a basis of equality with men. The Convention is legally binding.

To address gender issues in international education is to address the issue of progress of the implementation of the aims and principles of such a treaty. The treaty contains fourteen Articles. Together they explain what is expected for women in securing their share of civil rights and legal equality, the whole area of human reproduction, and the role of cultural factors in perpetuating discrimination against women. Article ten addresses the aims for education. Member states are committed to ensure that women have equal rights with men in the field of education. The eight aims are to provide

1. the same conditions for career and vocational guidance, with attention equally to rural and urban areas;
2. access to the same curricula, examinations, teaching staff and qualification standard and school premises and equipment of the same quality;
3. the elimination of any stereotyped concept of the roles of men and women at all levels and in all forms of education, by encouraging co-education and other types of education which will help to achieve this aim and, in particular, by the revision of textbooks and schools programmes and the adaptation of teaching methods;
4. the same opportunities to benefit from scholarships and other study grants;
5. the same opportunities for access to programmes of continuing education, including adult and functional literacy programmes,

particularly those aimed at reducing, at the earliest possible time, any gap in education existing between men and women;

6. the reduction of female drop-out rates and the organization of programmes for girls and women;
7. the same opportunities to participate actively in sports and physical education;
8. access to specific educational information to help ensure the health and well-being of families, including information and advice on family planning.

(United Nations,1989)

Individual countries are presented with a gargantuan task. The problem is one of legislative power, policies and ensuing practice. How does such a treaty become conventional in a real sense to people in everyday life? Where a country has adopted equal opportunity policies, practices will inevitably change to some extent, but in what way and to what degree? The central issue becomes one of discernment of progress in practice.

A further problem is that the rapid pace of change in recent years makes conditions difficult for "developing" and "developed" countries alike. The influences of the traditional, the modern and the postmodern coexist in different measure to make demands on the individual and upon education systems which serve them wherever they live. Gender issues arise in the complex interplay among these three influences. The constant factor is that girls and women face barriers in accessing different forms and levels of education. Once a woman has acquired the requisite credentials she often experiences fierce resistance to her entrance into the labour market on equal terms with men. Enlightened policies at the national level serve, potentially, to limit the effect of such barriers and to neutralize the effect of discriminatory practice at the local level. However, the relationship between educational achievement and subsequent employment remains an important but elusive one which merits due attention from researchers.

One might speculate that this relationship will fluctuate depending upon the dominance of traditional, modern or postmodern social, economic, and political influences. Where tradition predominates — as it so often does in "developing" countries — education focuses upon basic skills and labour is mostly craft-based. Modern influences have relied upon the development of an education system aimed at consistent performance in the workplace through the deployment of a variety of higher technological skills in industry, in business and in education. The current wave of interest in computer literacy within education itself is an example of this development. Women have learned to compete with men in the labour market. Postmodern influences bring experiential learning to the fore, with flexibility and specialization key factors in labour markets which are becoming increasingly fragmented. Women may well be advantaged by such developments or they may not.

The certainty and conformity of traditional ways of life, and the promise of emancipation, a significant feature of the modern world, may have given way to social, economic and political conditions of uncertainty and resistance in a postmodern world.

The commitment of the United Nations Convention to gender equity in education is a central concern of this book. Is practice congruent with policy, and vice versa? What do girls and women experience and are equal opportunity policies reducing discrimination in education?

It is here that we begin to explore with colleagues in Africa, Asia, Australia, North America and Europe this vexed question of the relationship between policy and practice in their countries and its effect upon the education of girls. Implementation of the policies to the benefit of girls and women, we maintain, will turn upon the congruity between stated national positions, in the form of equal opportunity policies in many cases, and resulting practice, the reality of everyday situations facing girls and women. Contributors were asked to consider the congruence or lack of it between such policy and practice in their country or region. From them we glean a measure of currently stated national agendas purported to be in the interest of women in education, and we see from the research a glimpse of the position in which girls and women find themselves. The position of education in each country reveals a measure of commitment to the United Nations Convention on the Elimination of All Forms of Discrimination Against Women.

In chapter 1, Margaret Sutherland clarifies the need to define more clearly the parameters of the nation-state in determining national policies. She gives a broad overview of the potential key players and agencies in policy formulation and signals both the possibilities and limits of governmental action.

In chapter 2, Eileen Turner, Sally Brown, and Sheila Riddell observe the development of policy and practice in Scotland, comparing and contrasting the stances taken by central and local authorities and schools along a continuum of minimum compliance to commitment to structural change. They analyse the tension among liberal, radical and feminist elements of policies and raise the issue of political backlash which can occur when equal opportunities are presented as more than the equal attainment of technological skills.

This issue is also taken up in the third chapter by Maggie Wilson and Hetty Dekkers, in which the very different experiences of the

Netherlands and England and Wales are examined. The more pro-active stance of the Dutch government from the 1970s onwards is contrasted with the laissez-faire position of the British government in terms of policy formulation. The crosscurrents of policy implementation in schools and in higher education are detailed and the tension between fulfilling short-term and long-term objectives is particularly highlighted.

In chapter 4, Jane Kenway, Peter Watkins, and Karen Tregenza consider new vocational agendas in schooling in the Australian education system. In particular, the chapter challenges the claim that boys are more at risk than girls in a changed economic climate and explores how the dislocation of labour markets affects the personal identities and social future of both sexes.

Nelly Stromquist tackles the interface between policy and legislation in the United States in chapter 5. Using the examples of two major pieces of legislation in the 1970s, she raises questions about the efficacy of the role of the state in promoting equal opportunities, as a source of strength or as a means of diluting an impetus for change. A similar theme in the Canadian context is taken up by Rebecca Coulter in chapter 6, who draws a distinction between policy and practice and policy with practice. The fragility of a positive equal opportunities policy at practitioner level in the province of Ontario and the effects of radical change of government are discussed in detail.

The final chapters move the issue of gender equality in education to the context of the "developing" world. In chapter 7, Karin Hyde provides a case study of Malawi, where barriers to girls' educational opportunities include traditional social attitudes and a lack of infrastructure, despite the surface commitment of the government. In chapter 8, Swarna Jayaweera summarizes the experiences of ten countries in East, Southeast and South Asia, contrasting different policy approaches to the question of girls' equal access to education. These are examined in relation to an unchanging domestic division of labour and rapidly changing labour-market participation.

Overview of the issues

Based on our experience of equal opportunity legislation in the United Kingdom, we have set out to learn what is happening in other countries. We challenge the view that legislation for equal opportunity in education in Britain, as elsewhere, has provided a wholly satisfactory improvement for girls in education.

Globally, the introduction of equality to education through legislation, education policy implementation, and equal opportunity policies is in practice problematic. The following chapters confirm this. Legislation per se is not necessarily effective. The implementation of policy, where it does exist, may not progress smoothly. The absence of compliance mechanisms is often as notable as their presence. Implementation can be affected adversely by an imbalance of social and economic interests. Active barriers may comprise cultural traditions, fluctuating labour market positions, and shifting political climates. All contribute towards the prospects and realities that face girls and women in daily life. Several chapters mention the relative acceptability of the "girls into science and technology" approach and the emergence of either hostility or inertia when policy initiatives depart from this. This illustrates that while a consensus can be built around gender policy constructed in terms of social efficiency, arguments based on social justice still fail to command the same degree of political purchase. More recent instances of radical conservative backlash against the promotion of equal opportunity for girls are documented in the American and Canadian contributions.

Although enlightened policies at government level serve potentially to limit the effect of such barriers and to neutralise the effect of discriminatory practice at local level, contributions alert us to the fact that where equal opportunity policies are in place they may be circumvented in ways which serve to minimise their impact.

In countries where a laissez-faire approach to the implementation of equal opportunity policies has been adopted, impetus may be lost over time, as illustrated in research from Scotland where teacher weariness and wariness are evident. Inertia may also develop as a result of inadequate resources for associated training and development due to financial constraints.

Largely absent at the national level is legislation which enables the translation of the humanitarian element of international rhetoric so desired by the United Nations Convention. Contributors demonstrate that inequalities continue in spite of legislation and policy. In countries traditionally dependent upon agricultural production or with a recent history of rapid industrialisation, traditional cultural attitudes may still result in the problem remaining one of gaining access to secondary or higher education. Access to the upper levels of education is a prerequisite to, but by no means guarantees, equality for women. The chapters on Malawi and South Asia describe the problem when education becomes a limited commodity and the education of boys is deemed a priority in the competition for places. The globalisation of economic operations and the unequal incorporation of women into the world market is a strong theme noted by researchers in this volume.

Even where the rhetoric of policy is one of true equality, girls face resistance in many forms in daily life, ranging from the subtle systematic discrimination of bureaucracy to the unbridled aggression of sexual harassment and worse. The Canadian contribution contextualises this in resistance to moves towards gender equality. This highlights the importance of attempts to develop anti-sexist strategies where work with boys is also considered to be a priority, as illustrated in the cases of the Netherlands and Canada.

While there is no doubt that education can provide the intrinsic rewards of personal development to girls and young women, the experience of school-leaving and entry into the labour market remains highly gendered, as particularly illustrated by the Australian case. The relationship between educational achievement of girls and women, and their fates in the labour market remains an important but elusive one which continues to engage attention of researchers, along with the continuance of the domestic division of labour.

The Global Strategy initiated in Beijing in 1995 by the United Nations Congress on Women, and supported by a Forum of Non-Governmental Organisations, placed, as stated earlier, a great responsibility upon education to effect an improvement in the lot of women generally. However, educational policies can help only when they are prepared to address gender issues of equality and social justice. In order to produce equal opportunity policies that can change the situation faced by girls, any global strategy must continually seek congruence between the humanitarian principles and equality in education. What is refreshing is that girls and women have come to expect more from their education systems. We hope that you will find these accounts as fascinating as we have and that as a result, you will address anew the prospects facing girls in education in your own land and worldwide.

Reference

United Nations. 1989. Women Discrimination Information Kit. New York: United Nations Department of Public Information, Economic and Social Programmes Section.

GENDER ISSUES IN INTERNATIONAL EDUCATION

CHAPTER 1

Evaluating National Policies on Gender Issues

Margaret B. Sutherland

In Beijing in 1995 the United Nations Congress on Women, supported by a Forum of Non-Governmental Organisations, produced a statement of a Global Strategy for improving the lot of women. Since this was by no means the first of the UN assemblies to discuss women's issues (these Congresses have been held at five-year intervals for some decades now), it may fairly be concluded that the situation of women still requires reform. It becomes the responsibility of the member states of the United Nations to accept and implement as government policy the changes indicated in the Beijing document.

Education is one of the major aspects for which the Global Strategy proposes reform. And yet for many years education has been the subject of a variety of governmental attempts to achieve the ideal provision. We may reasonably ask why at this time the need for new developments is proclaimed. What went wrong with earlier policies in education? Why have national policies apparently not succeeded?

If we are to evaluate national policies, we must of course define what we are evaluating. This is not as simple as we might expect; "national" is a wide and vague term; we have to recognise its different interpretations. Next comes the variety of methods by which attempts are made to put national policies into practice. We have to recognise also that a favourable or unfavourable outcome may depend largely on the means chosen for realisation of the policy rather than on the policy itself. Thirdly, if we evaluate, we must find appropriate criteria. How are we to judge the success of policies?

Definitions of National Policies

A national policy on gender issues can take widely different forms. In some countries national policy is said to be expressed in a written constitution. This indeed was the position in various countries under the Soviet regime; the constitution affirmed equality between men and women, so there appeared to be little need for a specific policy on gender. Even if a written constitution does not exist, we can easily take it for granted that a national policy is one defined by the government of a country. But the boundaries of countries or states are not necessarily the boundaries of nations. In some cases there are federal governments, responsible for a number of states or provinces as in, for example, the United States, Australia, and the Federal Republic of Germany. A federal policy is not necessarily identical with the policies favoured by individual members of the federation; and some federations accord greater autonomy than others to their individual components. They may indeed specifically leave to them the responsibility of determining policy in chosen aspects of social life; for instance, in Canada the central constitution leaves education as a responsibility of the individual provinces; consequently, each province can determine its own educational system. In Germany, while some educational principles are federally determined, each state (Land) has considerable freedom to decide its policy in education, for example in fixing the age and process of transition to secondary education. Thus in addition to federal policies there can coexist within federations a number of policies which could claim to be "national" in a more restricted sense.

Within federal states, or within less complex "national" states, authority for framing policies may also be delegated to subdivisions, to administrative units like counties or cities. For instance, until recent times it was happily claimed that in the United Kingdom there was a central policy for education which was locally administered; the permitted degree of interpretation of central policy was such that individual local authorities could claim to have their own policies, often associated with the political party which dominated them, hence sometimes diverging from the "national" policy of a government of a different political persuasion.

National policies are therefore not simply those expressed by central governments. Additionally, in various countries minority groups claim to speak for minority nations; for example Basques, Scottish, and Welsh nationalists demand respect for policies which they say are those of a nation distinct from the majority population. Such claims may highlight the tremendous differences in size which characterise "nations" — possibly the smaller the nation, the more vehemently its national policies are advocated. At the same time there is a probability that for such minority or threatened groups, the main emphasis on nationhood will blot out finer considerations of equality for women and men within the nation, just as resistance under an oppressive political regime in various countries, while depending on the support of women as well as men, has not necessarily brought about the equal participation of women in public affairs once liberation has been achieved. This kind of forgetfulness may be present in some European countries which have recently emerged from harsh political regimes but, on becoming a more democratic state, have not hastened to support equal rights for women (Kaplan 1992; Nash 1993).

Apart from vociferous statements about minority or oppressed "nations", views are also put forward by organisations representing a great number of people within a country and these also can be said to be national policies. Trade unions often propose a "national" policy for nationwide action; with regard to education, teachers' organisations similarly state policies they consider to be appropriate for the whole country.

More tenuously, if a "nation" is characterised by common values and aspirations, it could be said that these produce a kind of national policy, not written, not necessarily explicit, but motivating the behaviour of the majority of the population. Just as schools have a hidden curriculum, so countries may be said to have hidden policies.

Altogether, if we are evaluating national policies for gender equity, we must recognise that more than one national policy may be present in any chosen part of the world and that the policy of the central government may not necessarily be the policy which would be claimed as their own by the majority of the people of a country or group of countries. Conflict may be present among the policies offered to, or accepted by the people. Consequently the apparent importance of a "national policy" is less certain than the title suggests; such a policy may not in fact represent the general will. The question arises, is a centrally determined "national" policy likely to be more efficacious than national policies of the other kinds mentioned?

National and International Policies

Indeed, it is possible that the concept of a national policy peculiar to one country is becoming obsolete. Today national policies are increasingly influenced by consideration of the policies of other nations and by international pressures. Sometimes this influence is vague — it seems almost as if there is simply a general wish not to seem less virtuous or less enlightened than other governments. But at the most general level, the influence of UNESCO and of the United Nations itself guides individual governments towards policies which a number of nations have accepted as desirable. The United Nations Beijing Congress along with the Forum of Non-Governmental Organisations obviously represented a conscious attempt to shape and change individual countries' policies for equality of opportunity in many spheres, including education. (This assembly of non-governmental organisations also reminds us that international influences can also affect the policies of organisations within a country, such as trade unions and professional associations.)

Other international organisations also seek to influence policy and may increasingly have real effects on it. In Europe, for instance, the European Union issues Directives which are more or less dutifully accepted and followed by member states; in the matter of gender, the European Community affirmed already in 1976 "the principle of equal treatment for men and women as regards access to employment, including promotion and to vocational training, and as regards working conditions" (Social Europe 1991). (Since originally the European organisation was concerned with industrial relations, its emphasis has naturally fallen on employment conditions and on the kind of education associated with employment.) In the Community's Medium-Term Social Action Programme 1995–97, a key theme was again "equality of opportunity for men and women" and action was recommended for "reconciling working and family life, desegregating the labour market including reinforced access to training opportunities, and extending the principle of equal treatment, and promoting the concept of citizenship for women (gender balance in decision-making, strengthening of active citizenship)" (Social Europe 1995). This comprehensive policy does seem to merit universal adoption.

Similarly, the Council of Europe, which includes over forty European countries, has since 1949 influenced policy development in its member states by discussion in its Parliamentary Assembly and by various committees and conferences. It too has shown special concern for gender equity through the activities of its "Steering Committee for Equality between Women and Men" and its elaboration of the concept of "parity democracy", that is, affirming that equal representation and the participation of both gender groups are an essential characteristic of democracy (Olafsdóttir 1994).

The European Union has materially encouraged implementation of its preferred policies by awarding grants from its Social Fund for projects which are intended to improve women's access to training and employment and are proposed and partly funded by authorities within individual countries.

Another rather different form of international influence on national policies for gender equity, indeed a kind of international evaluation of national policies, is evident in the system by which individual cases are referred to the European Court of Justice (of the European Union) or to the European Court of Human Rights (Council of Europe). This kind of evaluation was exemplified in the Kalanke case of 1995 (Hoskyns 1996). This case arose in the state of Bremen. Because women were underemployed, a policy was set giving preference to women when job candidates of the opposite sex were equally well qualified. A man charged that this was discriminatory. The European Court ruled in his favour, finding that while steps could legitimately be taken to reduce women's disadvantages in finding employment, there could not be preferential treatment for women which would discriminate against men. The interpretations of this ruling were not immediately clear — they became the subject of much analysis — but undoubtedly the general effect was to make authorities in different European countries reconsider their own policies and be wary of policies which could be interpreted as unfair discrimination. International evaluation of this kind does not necessarily deal with a policy as a whole but it does try to determine whether in individual cases a policy — or the absence of a policy — has been unjust. Case law can thus become a feature of policy evaluation in the international sphere.

A milder form of intervention can be regarded as an alternative evaluation of national policies. Yearly since 1992, the OECD publishes *Education at a Glance*, reviews of statistics of different aspects of education in OECD countries. While this publication concentrates on reporting actual situations, data from different countries are juxtaposed and the comparisons which inevitably result must be expected to make individual governments aware of areas in which their provision seems inferior to that of other governments. The data collected include some evidence of results of policies for equality of females and males in education, showing whether educational policies are having the desired or intended effect. Future framing of policies, or the implementation of existing policies, should be materially affected by the information these reviews provide — assuming, that is, that members of governments pay intelligent attention to such publications and that they do not simply snatch from them a few unrepresentative figures to be used only to justify their own preferred policies.

Implementations of policies

Essentially the main forms of government action in trying to realise a policy are (1) legislation, (2) creation of special agencies, (3) dissemination of information to increase awareness of problems, and (4) promotion of research. The two latter categories of action, providing information and promoting research, are commonly included in the responsibilities of ad hoc agencies.

A major problem indeed is to decide which branch or branches of government should be involved in policy implementation, and whether it's better to have one specific agency or to entrust policy implementation to a number of governmental offices or agencies. Similarly, there is the question — as there is in framing a policy — whether many aspects of women's situation, such as health, employment, education and social participation, should be tackled at the same time, or whether a separate policy for one aspect alone is likely to be more effective. Since many of these aspects are interrelated, separation is difficult; yet attempting very wide reform may paralyse initiatives and overburden the responsible authorities.

Legislation

A relatively early example of federal governmental decisions to put policy into effect through legislation is to be found in the United States' law-making in 1972, where Title IX of its Education Amendment Act stated that "no person in the United States shall, on the basis of sex, be excluded from participation in, be denied the benefits of, or be subjected to discrimination under any educational programme or activity receiving Federal financial assistance." The Women's Educational Equity Act (WEEA) of 1974 enabled the financing of various projects to produce equality, including the development of teaching materials, research and teacher training. These two pieces of legislation exemplified also the contrasting way in which governments can seek to ensure that their policies are followed — by offering rewards (as in WEEA) or by imposing sanctions such as the loss of federal funding (Stromquist 1994). It is also to be noted that, unsurprisingly, financial support was recognised as vital. The degree of initial and continuing funding clearly has affected many policies: all too often the first impetus of implementation is lost as the amount of money made available is reduced in succeeding years.

In fact, in the United States the amount of money available for support of projects to improve equality in education tended to diminish in the years following the legislation. At the same time, it was noteworthy that many other United States organisations were acting in accordance with rather similar policies; there were in fact alternative "national" policies. Individual states passed their own laws on gender equity; parents' associations, in varying degrees, worked towards relevant reforms in their schools; publishers became concerned about the sexist content and language of materials used in education and issued their own guidelines to authors to enable them to avoid sexist nuances. Very obviously, legislation was not the only operative factor; policies of groups other than central government were striving for change — and, it must be recognised, policies of other groups were firmly against some of the changes proposed.

The use of legislation as the expression of a national policy for equal opportunities was evident in other countries in the same decade. In Denmark laws on equal pay and equal working conditions were passed in 1976 and 1978, and further use of legislation to promote greater opportunities for females was made in the 1985 Act to ensure equality of men and women as members of public bodies.

France similarly proceeded by legislation in its 1972 Law on Equal Pay and its 1983 Law on equal opportunities in employment, the latter seeking also to promote the production of action plans by large employers. In 1977 Sweden and Italy produced legislation for the removal of discrimination, a trend evident in various other Western European countries at the time. In the United Kingdom, similar legislation was found in the 1970 Equal Pay Act and the 1975 Sex Discrimination Act.

Generally, considerable legislative activity in those decades testified to increasing awareness of discrimination. Possibly at least some of this awareness and consequent policy developments can be attributed to the influence of the United Nations decision to declare 1973 "International Women's Year" and its nomination of the ensuing "Decade of Women". Admittedly it remains unclear what initiated this United Nations interest, whether the impulse came from some individual country or group of countries, or from other pressure groups.

Governmental agencies

To implement a policy of gender equity, an obvious step is to set up a government office or ministry with special responsibility for ensuring equality of opportunity. Spain, for example, established in 1983 its "Institute for Women", to study women's position and to raise awareness of inequalities. The example of France, however, may illustrate how difficult it apparently is to find the best kind of agency, for in the years between 1965 and 1985 it had a remarkable variety of committees, official secretariats and ministries. In 1965, a committee was formed to study the working conditions of women; in 1970, an information centre, followed by further variants in 1971 and 1972; then a state secretariat on women's situation; in 1978, a state secretariat in the Ministry for Employment; in 1982, a ministerial committee; in 1983, a higher council for vocational equality; and in 1985, a Ministry for Women (Cacouault and Zaidmann 1994). It is significant that in this instance also employment was regarded as a major sphere, requiring reform measures linking vocational education and equal chances for women and men in the labour market.

A rather distinctive kind of agency was set up by the United Kingdom to implement a policy for developing equality between males and females. This is the Equal Opportunities Commission (EOC), which was established by the 1975 Sex Discrimination Act. This Act did little to provide a policy for equality in education — education receives only limited mention in the Act itself — but the development of the EOC clearly showed recognition that widespread action was needed in education as well as in other spheres. The EOC's aims were stated to be the elimination of discrimination and the promotion of equal opportunities, reviewing provisions made by legislation, and responding to and reporting to the Secretary of State on relevant matters. The Commission's functions are extensive: investigating alleged discrimination; carrying out research and education; producing codes of practice for employers and others; monitoring health and safety legislation; carrying out enquiries; supporting individuals who claim to have been discriminated against; and producing various publications, including annual reports on the situation of women and men in Britain. It is to be noted that the responsibilities of the EOC are explicitly stated to be for both men and women. Indeed the number of men claiming to have been discriminated against in employment has in recent times equalled and surpassed the number of women. This, of course, does not prove that discrimination is greater in the one case than in the other. Much depends on the readiness of the individual to fight the case, and experience has shown that even when a complaint is successful, such action can cause considerable stress for the individual: men may be more ready than women to assert their rights even when the process is hurtful (Gregory 1989).

Yet again it has been noted (Hansard Society 1990) that funding for the EOC was already reduced, in real terms, in the 1980s. And public opinion, as expressed in the media, has not always been favourable to the EOC, whose actions have sometimes been portrayed as unrealistic and at an irresponsible extreme of feminism.

It is remarkable that while the EOC has, for good or for ill, become relatively well known for its concern with inequalities, there is also in existence in the United Kingdom another organisation specifically appointed to be concerned with the situation of women. This is the Women's National Commission (WNC), created in 1969 with a remit "to ensure by all possible means that the informed opinion of women is given its due weight in the deliberations of government" (WNC 1995). The implications of this wording are in themselves of considerable interest. The WNC is composed of representatives nominated by some eighty women's organisations (e.g., women's sections of political parties, professional associations, religious groups); it is provided with a small civil service secretariat and from 1992 came under the auspices of the Employment Department rather than, as at first, remaining in the Cabinet Office. Contact with the Cabinet is provided by an appointed co-chairman who is a government minister and works in the Cabinet subcommittee responsible for considering matters affecting women. From time to time the WNC appoints working groups to study and make recommendations about matters of concern to women. Publications of the WNC are readily available on request; yet its existence remains largely unknown to the general public. But in 1996 it joined with the EOC in producing a set of policy papers "In pursuit of equality", which analyses the proposals resulting from the Beijing Congress and indicate what actions should be taken, and which bodies — governments, NGOs, political parties — bear the responsibility for taking these kinds of action.

The U.K.'s two-pronged approach to reforming inequalities, by creating two rather different agencies, is perhaps indicative of the uncertainty regarding the ideal method of putting policy into practice. The interval between the creation of the two bodies was scarcely great enough to allow a shift in policy to develop. There are certainly noticeable differences in the financing of the two agencies and in the presence or absence of full-time specialist staff. There is also the likelihood that a group representing so many different organisations as the WNC may tend to be reactive rather than pro-active; and that the response to matters on which it is to give an opinion may lack unanimity. (In fact, the new Labour government decided in 1997 to review the WNC's functions.) More importantly perhaps, it is to be noted that whereas the WNC's remit is specifically to be concerned with women, the EOC is responsible for both genders, even if a large proportion of its work has addressed the inequalities suffered by females. It is fully possible that in the future, policies on gender issues will similarly attempt to be helpful to both gender groups and will have explicitly this dual function.

A useful reminder of the interlinking of different aspects of life in society and of the variety of problems which confront policies for equality of opportunity can be found in the Action Plan set out in 1989 by the Government of the Autonomous Region of Catalonia. In Spain as a whole, the new constitution of 1978 embodied the principle of non-discrimination between men and women, but this in itself was scarcely enough to eliminate traditional cultural attitudes. Since Spain gives its Autonomous Regions considerable freedom to determine their own policies in education, the government of Catalonia, referring with pride to the tradition of Catalonian women's struggles for emancipation at the end of the nineteenth century, approved in 1986 the proposal of its own Interdepartmental Commission for the Advancement of Women, and in 1989 approved that Commission's Action Plan.

The Plan merits special consideration, since it illustrates well the range of interlinked issues which are recognised internationally as of major importance in the lives of women. It had the advantage of being drawn up at a time when already there had been many discussions of gender issues and many publications of discussions on these topics. Its sections are

1. legal parity between men and women;
2. protective measures for women in desperate situations — mainly proposals for maintenance after divorce, income support for families with children, housing provision, and refuges for battered wives;
3. integrated protection for the family and for motherhood — this is mainly to safeguard the employment conditions of women workers who have children;
4. education based on equality;
5. fostering in society the appreciation of equalitarian values;
6. promoting the presence and active participation of women in society.

Education obviously was the subject of important proposals. Sexist content should be removed from textbooks. Teacher training must help teachers to overcome the sexist views they themselves are likely to have acquired, so that in the future they will be able to transmit equalitarian views — a point all too often overlooked by reformers. So far as the school curriculum is concerned, the introduction of domestic science for all pupils is seen as a way of eroding the traditional division of labour in society which has meant, in industrialised countries generally, that women have continued to be responsible for almost all household work, even if they are also working outside the home. Sex education courses are to be introduced to reduce the number of underage pregnancies and the undesirable attitudes found in many young people who are to be educated so that they will "conduct their sex lives in a responsible manner" (Action 24).

Parents' influence on the development of attitudes is recognised in the proposal for increased communication with parents' associations and work with them, so that attitudes favourable to equality may be disseminated among parents also.

The spread of co-education is referred to as likely to increase equality — a debatable point.

For the wider education of society, action is proposed in a variety of ways: support for women's participation in the Olympic Games (which were shortly to take place in Barcelona); and support for women's access to culture and to artistic expression, to vocational training and to the creation of business enterprises. Also to be promoted were research into the history of equalitarian movements in Catalonia; the avoidance of sexist use of language and monitoring the sexist or non-sexist presentation of advertisements in the mass media.

Unhappily, one impression which emerges most powerfully from these wide-ranging proposals is the well-justified and clear recognition of the strength and prevalence of sexist attitudes in society at the present time.

While the programme as a whole does seem admirably comprehensive, hopes of its implementation are perhaps slightly reduced by the discovery that responsibility for increasing women's participation in society is delegated to the Institute of Women, created to engage in the raising of awareness, to achieve publicity through its own publications as well as through the mass media and to maintain international contacts and give support to women's organisations.

While the Interdepartmental Commission had been created to heighten common awareness of the equality problems and to create a proposal of policy, nevertheless responsibility for implementing the proposed reforms was attributed by the Plan to a number of separate agencies: the Department of Education, of course, but also the Department of Health and Social Welfare, the Department of Labour, the Department of Economics and Finance, the Department of Justice, the Department of Industry and Energy, the Department of Trade, Consumer Affairs and Tourism, the Department of Land and Public Works, the

Home Office and the Presidency, and, as already mentioned, the Women's Institute of Catalonia. The recognition that so many departments have a part to play is important, as is the allocation of specific responsibilities to each, but there would seem to be a danger that the diversity of agencies may militate against a common commitment to ideals of equality and, possibly, evoke disagreement about the allocation of funds.

Positive Action: Information and Research

The best way to succeed may be with a narrow policy under the control of a single agency. As we have seen, education and employment are closely linked and various policies have emphasised the need to improve women's employment situation either through action at the employment level or by providing education which will improve employment chances. Obviously the two types of action complement each other. Australian policy for equality in women's employment has thus made clear links with women's and girls' education.

In 1986 Australian Commonwealth legislation produced the Affirmative Action (Equal Employment Opportunity for Women) Act. This laid on employers a responsibility for taking a series of clearly defined steps towards constructing and implementing policies to improve women's situation in employment. Thus employers must

1. produce a policy statement;
2. appoint someone to co-ordinate policy action;
3. consult with trade unions representatives;
4. consult employees concerning the policy;
5. draw up a profile of their own firm's personnel situation;
6. review their policies in appointment and promotion;
7. set objectives for improvement; and
8. monitor their progress towards these objectives.

The system was introduced gradually, beginning with employers having over one thousand employees and annually moving to include employers of smaller numbers of people. Annual reports have to be made to Parliament about compliance with the Act and reports are produced in Parliament to show those who are failing to satisfy the requirements of the legislation.

This kind of positive action is remarkable for its clearly defined programme and systematic, graduated steps for implementation. Its success, as yet, would seem to be partial since not all employers have complied with requirements. Yet many have in fact complied and their employees have benefitted accordingly. Moreover, educational establishments such as universities are also employers, so that the employment situation of women in higher education has been affected by this Act, as well as by the decision of individual universities to construct and implement their own policies for equal opportunities.

Two points may be noted apropos of the implementation of this ambitious piece of legislation. First, in Australia there are the problems of inequality based on ethnic group as well as on gender. Attempts to deal with a number of inequalities tend to be less rapidly and less completely successful than those uncomplicated by such conditions. Second, other recent developments in the Australian school system have drawn attention to the possibility that boys are becoming the disadvantaged group, being less successful in school exams and certificates than girls — it was scarcely envisaged that a policy of enabling girls to progress equally well would have this effect. At any rate, the widely publicised finding about the "poor boys" may reduce support for eliminating more important disadvantages suffered by females. Similar reactions have been noted in other places since, in developed countries, girls are often found to be more successful than boys in obtaining qualifications in upper secondary education (OECD 1992).

Evaluating Policies for Gender Equity: Successes and Failures

One major indication that policies have generally not been successful lies in the reports presented to and coming from the Beijing Congress. From these it is evident that the situation of females in education, health, legal systems, social welfare and societal decision-making is still unsatisfactory. While some countries report greater progress than others, few, if any, express confidence that equity has been achieved.

Developed and Developing Countries

Yet it must be recognised that real reductions in disadvantages have been made. In the developed countries of the world, access to primary and secondary education shows no disparities — or possibly, as just noted, some slight advantage on the female side in general secondary education. Similarly, access to higher education has become equally open for females and males. It is doubtful that this progress is due to policies consciously adopted in recent times, since decisions about equal access were made some time ago, even for access to universities. But although the doors of universities were opened to females at the end of the nineteenth century or the beginning of the twentieth, equal numbers of men and women did not immediately enroll. This equality would not occur for another fifty years or more. The eventual achievement of equal numbers entering higher education seems to have resulted not from explicitly declared policy but rather from changing economic conditions and especially from a shift, of unidentified origin, in public opinion in some countries from the 1960s onwards.

In some developing countries, though not in all, access to secondary and even to primary education is less open to females, even in countries where governments have stated policies of equal access. In some cases, such government policies have not yet conquered various financial problems, so education is not universally free — and parents see the education of boys as being more rewarding than the education of girls. Thus in addition to financial problems we find in some developing countries social attitudes which say girls do not need education. Such attitudes were, at earlier times, found in developed countries (and may still linger there). There is also a finding of some African research that secondary school girls, for various reasons, perform less well than boys (Gordon 1994). So in some countries governmental policy statements have not been enough; grass-roots policy has remained unaffected.

But not all developing countries can be said to show the same attitudes towards gender and to manifest the same gender inequalities. Research carried out by UNESCO's Regional Office for Asia and the Pacific found that in the Philippines, women surpassed men in entry to higher education and even at the postgraduate studies level; they were slightly under-represented in the administration of institutions of higher education, but had by 1985 achieved a forty percent representation in this area. In contrast, the work done in China and Nepal found women seriously under-represented in access to higher education, at both undergraduate and postgraduate levels. Although in China the official policy of the communist state was for equality, it was found that considerable traditional attitudes militated against women's progress. In Nepal, evidence of such opposition by tradition was even stronger. In the Philippines, admittedly, there was also evidence of some traditions opposed to women's progress and there was continuing concern for their role as mothers. Apparently, progress was made — not because of legislation or official policy but rather because of an important change in social attitudes, allowing access for women to higher education and to positions of responsibility in society (UNESCO 1990).

An interesting example of contradictions between explicit and implicit national policies can also be cited in Sri Lanka, where the legislation for access to education did indeed help towards equality of opportunity for females. Unfortunately, the lack of awareness on the part of policy-makers concerning the "hidden curriculum", the social pressures towards gender-biased vocational choices, meant that women's role in economic production was not recognised and that women's role in society's decision-making continued to be restricted (Jayaweera 1994).

An indication of the need for more effective implementation of policies of gender equity even in developed countries is found when we consider information relating to women's presence as postgraduate students and as teachers and administrators in higher education. Many publications, notably "The Gender Gap in Higher Education" (Lee and Malik 1994), have shown that in a wide range of countries, even where women achieve entry to undergraduate studies in numbers equal to those of men — or even in slightly greater numbers than men — they become minorities again at the postgraduate, especially at the doctoral, level. Again, such studies repeatedly show that women are in a minority among teachers in higher educational establishments, especially at the top professorial levels. Women also remain rare among the top-level administrators in higher education and among members of research councils. Responsibility for this situation cannot be attributed to a formal policy; it stems rather from possibly unproclaimed traditional policies.

We find too, in probably every country, gender bias in the choices of subjects of study — and hence of professions. While freedom of choice apparently exists, and while we cannot assume that men and women are equally attracted to the same studies, it is reasonable to think that there are social pressures, traditions, expectations, matters of availability of employment, which constrain this freedom of choice. Official policies for equality have failed to cope effectively with these implicit policies.

Similar structures, showing women under-represented at top levels, have been found in many professions, in many countries, as has the sex-segregated nature of the labour market.

Political Decision-Making

If national or international policies for gender equity are to be effectively formulated and implemented in education and in other aspects of society, it would seem essential that women participate in the creation of these policies. Yet we find that women are distinctly in the minority in policy-making bodies, in national parliaments, in the

European Parliament, in the European Commission — and at top levels in UNESCO and the United Nations.

It is true that in recent times efforts have been made in some countries and in international organisations to arrive at a more equitable proportion of women in top administrative posts and some countries' policies have achieved success here. We find, for example, that by 1994 Denmark had 43.8 percent women among its Members of the European Parliament; Germany, Spain, Luxembourg, the Netherlands and Belgium had each achieved over 30 percent (and France, 29.8) (Hoskyns 1996), but Greece, Italy, Portugal and the United Kingdom had less than 20 percent women MEPs. The picture is rather less encouraging when members of the national parliaments are considered. Denmark and the Netherlands still lead with over 30 percent, but apart from Germany with 25.6 per cent, none of the other countries has over 20 percent women members of parliament and four have fewer than 10 percent. Overall the percentage of women in the European Parliament in recent times has been 25.7 percent and in parliaments of the member states of the European Union, 12.3 percent.

Of course it has to be recognised that in some countries outside the European Community as good if not better progress has been made in electing women; for example, Norway has achieved almost equal representation of women at the Cabinet level. Yet it has also been noted that with the overthrow of the Soviet regimes in European countries, the percentage of women in their parliaments has dropped — an indication that the Soviet policy of quotas did indeed have some effect (Nash 1993).

From these various successes and failures we may deduce both the ineffectiveness of national or international policies to achieve rapid or complete reform and note the effectiveness of the implicit policy, the popular policy embodied in traditions and attitudes — and in some cases, the policy of individual political parties or women's organisations for needed reforms.

Yet another illustration of the conflict between official policies and policies implicit in tradition may be found in Japan where the new constitution introduced in 1946 after defeat in the Second World War explicitly affirmed the equality of women and men, and boys' and girls' equal rights to education. The Fundamental Law of Education in 1947 again reaffirmed equal opportunity, non-discrimination on the grounds of "sex, race, creed or social status, economic position or family origin" (Kamijo 1994) and — presumably with a view to ensuring equal opportunity, and influenced by the American model which was then dominant — introduced co-education. Yet while it is true that female completion of upper secondary education is rather better than that of males (92.8 percent versus 86.3 percent of the relevant age populations (OECD 1992), very considerable differences still exist in the kind of higher education to which the two gender groups then proceed. While most male students enter full universities, most female students go to higher education institutions giving shorter courses; thus in the relevant age population, 14.4 percent of women and 37.7 percent of men achieve a first degree (OECD 1992). There is also very strong gender bias in the kind of studies undertaken, and it is widely recognised that women are much less likely than men to proceed to high-ranking positions in industry, commerce, or politics (Stockman, Bonney, and Xuewen 1995). Further attempts have been made to try to improve the general education situation of females. The National Women's Centre was founded in 1977 to promote continuing education for women, and the Women's Bureau of the Ministry of Labour has been attempting to raise awareness of women's working conditions and wider social participation. In 1989 amendments made to the centrally-determined curriculum were intended to reduce gender bias (Kamijo 1994). Yet despite many attempts to remedy the situation through legislation, and through government agencies and ministries, it is evident that in Japan, as in other countries the implicit policy of society has succeeded to a great extent in maintaining the traditional role of women.

Conclusions

Overall, some progress is evident, especially when we consider the gradual evolution of attitudes in many countries, even in those where change is slow to come. The tempo of such change in Europe and in other countries may of course also be attributed to their past political life, those which have been free from oppression by radical or dictatorial governments having apparently been better able to move towards greater social equality for women (Kaplan 1992).

We may note also, as perhaps a contributing factor — or evidence of attitude change — the introduction of Women's Studies into various forms of education, especially in higher education establishments. This certainly is a change which has not come about because of a central policy — though it has been helped in Scandinavian countries and in the Netherlands by government financial support for lecturing posts and for research. In principle it has been due to individual initiatives and to informal agreement among interested and aware individuals and groups.

In general, from this survey, we must conclude that legislation and governmental agencies have not been sufficient to make policies of gender equity effective. What has repeatedly emerged as important is the goodwill of the population in the part of the world in question. Financing is certainly another important factor, but money-spending does depend on the willingness of the population to accept the use being made of economic resources. Governments are most likely to give financial support and make serious efforts to implement a policy when they are aware that this is in accordance with the general will of the population. While some governments may engage in a window-dressing exercise by passing legislation or by appointing special agencies in order to keep up with international fashions, if not convinced of genuine popular support for a policy, legislators can easily delay putting law into practice, and/or refuse the funding necessary for policy implementation, and fail to give adequate support to their own special agencies or ministries. Policy must come from and be supported by people at the grass-roots level.

References

Cacouault, M., and C. Zaidmann. 1994. Les politiques nationales concernant la formation des femmes: le cas de la France. In M.B. Sutherland and C. Baudoux eds. *Femmes et Education: Politiques Nationales et Variations Internationales*. Quebec: Université Laval, 11–42.

Gordon, R. 1994. National policy for the education of women and girls in Zimbabwe. In Sutherland and Baudoux, op. cit., 371–96.

Government of Catalonia, 1989, *Action Plan for the Equality of Opportunities for Women*. Barcelona: Institut Català de la Dona.

Gregory, J. 1989. *Trial by Ordeal*. London: HMSO

Hansard Society, 1990. *Women at the Top*, London: The Hansard Society for Parliamentary Government.

Hoskyns, C. 1996. *Integrating Gender: Women, Law and Politics in the European Union*. London & New York: Verso.

Jayaweera, S. 1994. National policies for the education of girls and women in Sri Lanka. In Sutherland and Baudoux, op. cit., 299–325.

Kamijo, M. 1994. Comparative study of national policies for the education of girls and women: The situation of Japan. In Sutherland and Baudoux, op.cit., 243–297.

Kaplan, G. 1992. *Contemporary Western European Feminism*. London: UCL Press.

Lee, S. and L. Malik. 1994. The gender gap in higher education. *World Yearbook of Education*. London & Philadelphia: Kogan Page.

Nash, M. ed. 1993. From Dictatorship to Democracy: Women in Mediterranean, Central and Eastern Europe. Conference Report. Barcelona: University of Barcelona.

Organisation for Economic Cooperation and Development (OECD). 1992. *Education at a glance.* Paris: OECD.

Olafsdóttir, O. 1994. Intergovernmental cooperation in the field of equality between women and men in the Council of Europe. In *Report of Wolfheze Conference on Equality and Partnership towards Higher Education, Employment/Entrepreneurship and Environmental Management in Central and East European Countries.* Zoetermeer, The Netherlands: European Network of Scientific and Technical Cooperation on Women's Studies.

Social Europe. 1991. *Equal opportunities for women and men.* Luxembourg: Commission of the European Communities.

Social Europe. 1995. *Medium-term social action programme 1995–97.* Luxembourg: European Commission.

Stockman, N., N. Bonney and S. Xuewen. 1995. *Women's Work in East and West.* London: UCL Press.

Stromquist, N. 1994. State policy and gender equity in U.S. In Sutherland and Baudoux, op.cit., 11–42.

UNESCO, Principal Regional Office for Asia and the Pacific. 1990. *Women's Participation in Higher Education: China, Nepal and the Philippines.* Bangkok: UNESCO Principal Regional Office for Asia and the Pacific.

Women's National Commission. 1995. *Women in the 90s.* London: Women's National Commission.

CHAPTER 2

Gender Equality in Scottish Schools: The Rhetoric of Policy And the Reality of Practice[1]

Eileen Turner, Sally Brown and Sheila Riddell

Introduction

This chapter is concerned with how the various strands of policy associated with gender equality relate to the practice of school education in Scotland. There are very obvious variations and discontinuities across the country and between different aspects of policy and practice. While all the features considered in this account could be said to be pursuing "equal opportunities" in the broad sense of promoting equal treatment of women and men within social institutions, there is strong evidence for variability in the ways in which problems of gender equality and strategies for change are conceptualised. One way of looking at this is to trace the influence of different kinds of feminist theories on those conceptualisations. In this case, we have taken the approaches characterised by Eisenstein (1984), cited by Acker, (1994), as radical, socialist and liberal feminism as the general framework for making comparisons.

Recent analysts seem to agree on the distinction between radical feminism, which holds that gender oppression is the oldest and most profound form of exploitation, which pre-dates and underlies all other forms including those of race and class; and socialist feminism, which argues that class, race and gender oppression interact in a complex way, that class oppression stems from capitalism, and that capitalism must be eliminated for women to be liberated. Both of these, in turn, would be distinguished from a liberal or bourgeois feminist view, which would argue that women's liberation can be fully achieved without any major alterations to the economic and political structures of contemporary capitalist democracies (Eisenstein 1984, pp. xix–xx).

The Scottish context in which this research was undertaken reflected what has traditionally been a fairly centralised system. That system is distinctive from those of countries making up the rest of the United Kingdom, although there have been similarities in legislation and innovation over the last few years. Responsibility for formulating and implementing policy rests with the Scottish Office Education and Industry Department (SOEID) and Her Majesty's Inspectorate (HMI) in Edinburgh, rather than the Department for Education and Employment (DfEE) and the Office for Educational Standards (OFSTED) in London. The powerful influence of the Scottish Certificate of Education (SCE), which has been the responsibility of the single Scottish Examination Board (SEB), has ensured that something like a national curriculum was in place in Scottish secondary schools long before education in England had a centralising framework imposed upon it. The advent in the 1990s of national curriculum guidelines in Scotland was much less disruptive, therefore, than was the case south of the border.

Responsibility for operation of schools within the state maintained sector has rested largely with the local education authorities. Until local government re-organisation, which took place in 1996, nine Regional Councils and three Islands Authorities had responsibility for the provision of education in Scotland. While some of their control has been eroded through the devolution of budgetary control to schools (Devolved School Management), education authority influence on educational practice in Scotland (unlike England) remained significant. From 1979 until 1997 the United Kingdom had a Conservative government. In 1992, however, only 26 percent of the Scottish population voted Conservative, reflecting a local government pattern in which other political parties, notably the Labour Party and the Scottish National Party, were in power. In some authorities there was "no overall control," while elsewhere "Independents" controlled the councils. Not one of the twelve education authorities was in Conservative hands. This was clearly a potential source of trouble; however, a measure of what is often called "consensus", but is in reality a readiness to compromise, has ensured that the Scottish educational debate has been less acrimonious than that in England over the last few years. Partnerships among central government, education authorities and schools have been evident (albeit somewhat uneasy).

We look first at the policy stances of those aspects of the system providing the context in which the education authorities work. By the contextual aspects we mean the main teachers' union, the Educational Institute of Scotland; the General Teaching Council for Scotland (GTC); and the Scottish Office Education and Industry Department (SOEID). The GTC has responsibility for maintaining standards of teaching in

Scotland and the SOEID is essentially a ministry of education for Scotland within the larger United Kingdom.

We then address education authorities' equal opportunities policies directly, suggesting a way of categorising them on a continuum ranging from those promoting minimal compliance with legal requirements to those which seek structural transformation of the whole system. This section leads into a third, which is concerned with how gender equality issues are dealt with in practice. The final section looks at the overall picture of this important feature of schooling in Scotland and at the theoretical underpinning of policy and practice.

Policy Background for Educational Authorities

Teachers' Union

As a result of a report presented to, and agreed upon by, the 1989 Annual General Meeting of the Educational Institute of Scotland (EIS, the largest teachers' union in Scotland), equal opportunities leaflets were produced (EIS 1990a and b) "as a positive assertion against sexism" (quotation attributed to the EIS General Secretary). The report itself (EIS 1989) took a similar stance, stating: "For EIS members, passive support for equal opportunities will not be enough. The real and legitimate aim for members will be the *challenging of institutional sexism*" (para. 1.14, p. 3 italics ours). The report drew attention to many disparities, suggesting that schools contributed to "the reproduction of the gender inequalities of our society" (para. 3.1.2, p. 3) since boys

- demand and receive a generous share of teacher time;
- receive a disproportionate share of hands-on experience (e.g., in science or computing);
- receive apologies from teachers when asked to undertake non-traditional tasks;
- are rewarded for being assertive;
- are advised not to act like girls;
- receive a disproportionate share of coveted class materials (para.3.2.5, p. 5).

The report further argued that EIS members should understand that an effective anti-sexist education requires more than equal opportunities for girls. It must challenge the gender assumptions of boys and the self-image of all pupils. (para 3.6.1.(7), p. 9).

Of around 50,000 teachers in Scotland in 1989, 43,685 were members of the EIS (about two-thirds of these were women). With such numbers, one might have expected this policy to have made a big impact in schools, especially in the primary sector where the union predominates. However, few respondents in our research referred to it unless prompted. It is not clear what efforts have been made by the EIS to monitor the implementation of its policy. An ad hoc Committee on Anti-Sexist Policy has been updating the 1990 document and two sections, "Countering Sexism in Education" and "Countering Sexism in Education at Work and in the Union," were completed by November 1996 (EIS 1996).

The General Teaching Council

In December 1991, the General Teaching Council for Scotland (GTC) published *Gender in Education*. This policy document reviewed the impact of the Sex Discrimination Act (1975) and commented on the limited amount of improvement that had occurred over fifteen or so years. In a particularly graphic phrase the point was made that, in seeking equal opportunities, girls should not be seen as "deficient boys" to be turned into "surrogate males" (p. 4). Four areas for future action were identified:

1. the curriculum: content, resources and image;
2. course choice, careers guidance and counselling;
3. school ethos and teacher attitude;
4. staff development and training (p. 5).

The point was made that it is never too early to start raising awareness; children commonly enter nursery schools with gender stereotypical attitudes already in place.

This document, which took a fairly pro-active stance, aroused mixed feelings among the respondents to our study. While a few teachers and officials regarded it as influential and helpful, others seemed unaware of its existence and some thought it far too strident. It is perhaps worth noting that the generation of the document within the GTC owed much to the views and tenacity of one woman, the then Depute Registrar. While Council members (including a majority of teachers) supported the document, it has been suggested that without her determination and commitment, this policy statement would probably have had lower priority.

The Official Scottish View

A triumvirate of organisations with almost exclusively male senior managements — the Scottish Office Education and Industry Department, the Scottish Examination Board, and the Scottish Consultative Council on the Curriculum (SCCC) — continue to control and influence Scottish schooling (Macintosh 1993; Hills 1990). The issue of gender is raised rarely in their publications. Exceptions include the SCCC's cross-curricular pack (SCCC 1993), two other documents issued around the same time (SCCC n.d. a, b), and research bulletins produced by the SEB from time to time (e.g., SEB 1995). The SEB provides guidelines for question setters on the use of gender neutral language and the choice of appropriate contexts and examples and has established checking procedures to see that marking and other assessment procedures are free from bias. The Scottish Office Education Department (SOED, forerunner of the SOEID) issued, between 1991 and 1993, a series of documents known as "National Guidelines" to support the "5-14 programme" (the Scottish national curriculum). The earlier documents in this series (e.g. Guidelines for English, SOED 1991a; and Mathematics, SOED 1991b) required teachers to cater for the needs of individual pupils, but made no specific reference to gender. Later, the Guidelines on 'reporting' (SOED 1992) included a single page on "gender issues" under the general heading of "promoting equality of opportunity." This section directed teachers' attention to a number of questions to teachers:

- Are girls and boys praised equally for progress across all areas of the curriculum or are they more often praised for traditional female/male activities?
- Are personal aspects interpreted in the report in the same way for boys and girls?
- Are girls more often rewarded for passive and boys for active behaviour? (SOED, 1992, p. 31)

The inclusion of this material was a considerable departure for SOED publications. It was in stark contrast with the extraordinary paucity of references to gender issues in published reports of school inspections by Her Majesty's Inspectorate (HMI). HMI has a responsibility for monitoring and reporting on standards, policies and practices in Scottish schools. Through a system of inspection visits, inspectors offer advice to individual schools on how specific problems might be addressed, but also collate findings from many inspections into general published reports. They additionally are charged with responsibility for the introduction and successful implementation of centrally determined innovations in curriculum, assessment and pastoral care. If gender equality was seen by HMI as important, it would be expected that either good practice or neglect of such matters would be cause for comment in areas such as curriculum, staffing or behaviour.

The Equal Opportunities Commission, responding to this neglect in its 1995 "agenda setting" review of education and training in Scotland, suggested that it would "press the Scottish Office Education Department, through Her Majesty's Inspectorate, to place equal opportunities provision in primary and secondary schools on the agenda for inspection and for reporting" (EOC 1995, p. 17).

There have been further indications of a lack of official attention to gender equality issues. Evidence of an educational system where "gender inequality is embedded" and gender bias has "been largely unrecognised" (Fewell and Paterson 1990, pp. 1-2) is all too obvious in published statistics. SOEID's own figures (1994) show, for example, that there were only 18 female headteachers in 394 secondary schools in Scotland; with the recent increase (April 1996) in the number of education authorities to 32, only 5 women have been appointed as directors of education. Yet the SOEID has no formal equal opportunities policy directive, and gender equality, as we discovered in a series of interviews with a sample of Chief Inspectors, has had a very low profile. At the time of these interviews (1995) there was only one woman among thirteen Chief HMIs, and none of our respondents was able to identify a senior colleague with responsibility for equal opportunities in the schools' sector. Subsequently, we learned that such responsibility did exist within the Inspectorate, but the ignorance of it among senior members adds emphasis to our point. It is difficult not to conclude that government thinking in this area is limited, purely reactive, and without any sense of strategic vision.

Gender Equality Policies Of Scottish Education Authorities

A Continuum of Policy Positions

By 1995, when the research was undertaken, most of the twelve educational authorities had published an equal opportunities policy statement, though these varied from one- or two- page documents to substantial publications. Some had prepared a brief form for easy access; others supported the policy with detailed implementation guidelines. A few authorities had a separate gender policy statement; but in most cases gender was one aspect of an all-encompassing equal opportunities policy. In some urban areas, multicultural and anti-racist education issues featured more strongly than gender issues. Less emphasis, generally, was placed on inequalities resulting from social class and disability. The most striking feature was how recently most of the policy statements had been formulated (see figure 1). Figure 1 summarises this information about the development of equal opportunities policies and implementation guidelines. To preserve anonymity the letters A–L have been randomly allocated to the education authorities. Appendix 1 provides additional contextual details about the authorities.

Figure 1. Equal Opportunities: Policy and Guidelines Development in Scottish Education Authorities

Authority	Was there a policy?	Date (if known)	Were there Guidelines?	Comments
A	No		Yes	Guidelines produced under TVEI, 1992
B	Yes	1994	Included in policy	Policy merges 3 former policy statements
C	Yes	1991	Yes	Guidelines compiled 1992
D	Yes	1991	Yes	Guidelines compiled 1992
E	Yes		No	
F	Yes		No	Very brief statement
G	Yes	1990	Included in policy	
H	Yes	1994	Not detailed	Draft version only
I	Yes		16 points as annex to policy	1 page only but covered by council's overall employment policy
J	In process		Being prepared	
K	In process		Much material produced since late eighties	All aspects of EO covered in 1 document
L	Yes	1990	Yes	Guidelines issued October 1994

Generally, the documents had been developed by small teams or committees drawn from the authority and its schools. There was, in most cases, no representation of parents, pupils or unions. The development process frequently received support from the Technical and Vocational Education Initiative (TVEI). This central government initiative, operating from the mid-1980s, had for the first time explicitly made secondary schools aware of, and accountable for, some aspects of gender in curricular provision.

It is interesting to recall that TVEI received its funding and impetus, not from the educational establishment, but from the Manpower Services Commission and was to a large extent motivated by an economic, rather than an educational rationale. A great deal of extra resources were directed into Scottish schools during the late eighties and early nineties, some of which were earmarked for gender-related activities such as awareness-raising courses for staff and students, the formulation of equal opportunities policies and the production of classroom materials, but only in the secondary sector.

The content of the policies varied considerably across authorities. We characterised equal opportunity policies on a continuum from conservative "laissez-faire" approaches (ensuring minimal compliance with legal requirements) to radical initiatives implying "structural transformation" (see figure 2). These categories were not mutually exclusive, rather they overlapped. We identified examples of "positive action", such as "women into management courses" or particularly committed individual teachers, in some of the authorities which were placed towards the "laissez-faire" end of the continuum.

Figure 3 shows the approximate position of each education authority on the continuum and demonstrates that a majority were situated towards the "laissez-faire", "open-door" end.

Those which tended towards "positive action" and "structural transformation" served predominantly large urban populations and were politically left of centre. At the "structural transformation" end of the continuum education authorities gave very clear indications of commitment to equality. Authority C, for example, stated in the introduction to its "Code of Practice (gender)," "These practices seek to demonstrate specific commitment to gender equality and to create an appropriately supportive climate."

The spokesperson for Authority D, when asked whether its policy could be characterised as "positive action" replied, "Yes, I think that we have to be. There is a range of different views. If we identify, by monitoring, things which do not meet our guidelines, we have to act, to

Figure 2: The policy continuum

It is possible to characterise EA Equal Opportunity policies as:

Laissez Faire — The authority minimally complies with equal opportunities legislation over access to the curriculum and employment etc. but seeks to do little more.

Open door — The authority publicises opportunities for all but does not try to influence choice. An individualistic approach which might be characterised as a weak EO position. Often associated with quantitative measures e.g. encouraging girls to take science, technology through, TVEI, WISE etc.

Positive Action — The authority makes efforts to reverse trends which lead to gender (or other) inequality e.g. awareness — raising activities, single sex management courses; provision of facilities such as job sharing, crèches. Might be characterised as a strong EO approach.

Structural transformation — The authority is concerned with equality of outcome as well as opportunity. Emphasis placed on identifying institutional factors contributing to inequality. A collectivist approach marked by a concern with relationships, sexuality and economic outcomes. The concept of 'social justice' underlines many strategies. Involvement of pupils, parents, other groups may be encouraged.

Figure 3. The Location of Education Authorities on The Policy Continuum

Authority	Laissez faire	Open door	Positive action	Structural Transformation
A	→			
B		→		
C				→
D			→	
E			→	
F	→			
G		→		
H		→		
I	→			
J		→		
K				→
L				→

Note: See Appendix 1 for a profile of identifying letters.

take positive action. Positive career counselling, the positive career support model for women and networks are clear examples of positive action. But we also have to take positive action with those who are interviewing, those who are writing references."

Such a commitment, however, often implied a fairly directive approach on the part of the authorities. Authority K's newly formulated policy, for example, was said to place emphasis on "positive action" because it had been found that an "open-door" approach had not worked. And an official from Authority L, in claiming that "positive action is implicit in all the policies," admitted that such an approach could cause resentment as many people needed "help with the concept."

At the other end of the spectrum, the spokesperson for Education Authority F, one of three remote Islands Authorities, characterised its position as "a laissez-faire policy. The kinds of responses we get when we start talking about equal opportunities range from the very positive right through to the completely negative."

The policy document for Authority I stated that: "[i]t is a legal requirement to stop discrimination on grounds of race, culture, religion, sex and disability, and to ensure that facilities for education are provided without direct or indirect discrimination." The same policy document states that "the purpose of this paper is to assist schools and colleges to promote through formal, informal and hidden aspects of the curriculum a climate conducive to the provision of equal opportunities for all."

A policy of this kind can be characterised as minimalist and as paying "lip service" to the legal requirements, but little more. It shares features with what Farish et al. (1995) described, at an institutional level, as belonging to "first-time-around policies." Virtually no attempt is made to take action to advance the education or employment opportunities of under-represented groups, consciousness of problems is episodic and strategic thinking largely absent.

The policies of some other authorities, especially those which had been developed only recently, did not look much beyond curricular access (the numbers game) and the removal of sexist language from learning materials or reading schemes which perpetuated gender stereotypes. A spokesperson from one authority reported that the main motivation for its equal opportunities policy had been pressure from TVEI aimed at "getting girls into non-gender stereotypical jobs"; there was a perception "that there was a skill shortage" and that women constituted "a pool of wasted talent." This economic rationale provided a somewhat cynical interpretation of equal opportunities when compared with the social justice arguments found elsewhere, but such a rationale was regarded by the education authorities as practical. The focus was clearly on girls and women changing their attitudes, aspirations and behaviour to fit the status quo. The spokesperson from another authority argued similarly.

> The reason, particularly the governmental reason, for that at that time was to ensure a flexible workforce approach .... In trying to develop non-stereotypical work experience placements we targeted girls in particular. We were getting girls into what were seen as 'boys' jobs.

Few education authorities addressed issues like classroom management, teaching and learning approaches, relationships and other aspects of equality within their policy statements. In several authorities, we were told, gender issues and equal opportunities were expected to be covered within social education programmes. It seems unlikely, however, that these included broader concepts of gender matters such as sexual harassment and sexuality; none of these was spontaneously mentioned by respondents. Only one policy document specifically referred to sexual orientation (Authority L, near the structural transformation end of the continuum), while three others mentioned grievance procedures to be followed if sexual harassment occurred.

Spokespersons from rural Authority A (laissez faire) felt that our categorisation was inappropriate in their case. "We concentrate on the needs of the individual and the rest will take care of itself," they reported. "We are not into positive discrimination in any way. It could be very counter-productive here to have a specific gender focus."

The conclusion that we drew from this part of the study, however, was that although a concern with the needs of individuals can complement an "open-door" "social-justice" approach to equality, when the approach is used alone it often results in a lack of attention being paid to group needs. We found further references to the individual-needs approach at school level across the country, especially in the primary sector, and these tended to lead to the neglect of gender issues which appeared not to "take care of themselves".

Monitoring and evaluation of policy implementation

The process of monitoring seemed to be at a very early stage of development with many authorities still considering how evaluation might be undertaken. Authority K (towards the structural-transformation end of the continuum) had probably advanced furthest with what a spokesperson suggested was a monitoring system "unique in Scottish terms." It had established a quality-assurance unit which conducted annual "inspections" of a large number of educational establishments and published reports. The authority's mission statement indicated that in aiming to offer "education of the highest quality" it would seek to:

- provide a full range of courses and services;
- enable all individuals to achieve their potential;
- supply suitable premises and resources;
- encourage access to education throughout life;
- foster genuine partnership in education;
- promote equal opportunity and social justice; and
- support economic growth and prosperity.

Evaluation reports were prepared using these headings. In 1994 this authority had published a *Survey of the Provision for Equal Opportunities*, for which it had canvassed the views of 30,000 parents. Another spokesperson stressed that it was essential to monitor "not only what teachers, and other staff, **do** but the effect that it has on the learner." Their monitoring procedures had been devised, therefore, to cover not only aspects of educational provision but also prescribed outcomes, and the impact on learners. Some of these outcomes were quantitative measures, for example, examination performance and truancy; it was more difficult, however, to devise ways of evaluating pupils' feelings of being respected and valued, which were regarded as important indicators of successful policy implementation. Experiments with self-evaluation techniques were continuing.

In authorities where monitoring systems were in place, some form of audit was the most common mechanism used. Another technique was the use of rolling programmes of reports and inspections. Authority C (structural transformation) planned to develop "quality indicators" for schools to use in self-review and for follow-up monitoring by teams from the region's quality-assurance division. School Development Plans (SDP), all of which were expected to include equal opportunities, were seen as a further way of monitoring. Scrutiny of SDPs was also the favoured mechanism for review in Education Authority L (structural transformation). However, most authorities, especially those at the laissez-faire end of the continuum, had introduced no formal mechanisms for monitoring and evaluation.

Personnel and practice

An examination of the locus of responsibility for this aspect of education again revealed a continuum of practice ranging from Authority A (laissez-faire) which had nobody nominated to deal with equal opportunities ("you were directed to me because I am the only female member of the Directorate"), to a special five-person "Equality Education Team" in predominantly urban Authority C (structural transformation) with a Labour-controlled council. There were almost as many patterns of personnel deployment as there were education authorities. The key role played by specific individuals was often highlighted. In Authority L (structural transformation) much progress in respect to equal opportunities policy development was attributed to "the strong influence" of the director of education, who had dealt with equality issues and generated substantial activity while in her previous post of senior depute director. A spokesperson from Authority K (structural transformation) dated the development of gender awareness there from the arrival in post of a particular directorate official; "the advent of [X] as depute. He became the line manager .... set up a structure of committees." This official was seen to have exhibited a level of commitment which had not been evident in his predecessors.

Considerable importance was placed on the interaction of such high-level commitment with the major role played by grassroots professional teachers. In one authority, we were told that "over the last 5 to 10 years teachers' views have changed." In Authority D (positive action) a male senior depute director had chaired a group which had worked on the authority's equal opportunities policy, which covered gender, race, disability and class. The involvement of such a senior person was indicative of the importance placed on the issue of equality by the authority as a whole. It was seen as something of which everyone had to take account. This official stressed the value of having, alongside movements from the grassroots and demands for action, "people within the directorate who feel very strongly about it and who are keen to be pro-active about it, I think that is an important parallel factor. I would be seen as veering towards the fanatical on this subject."

The importance of a groundswell of interest from classroom teachers being complemented by movement from the top was a strand which ran through all the research findings. A theme which also emerged from the interviews with authority spokespersons was the extent to which progress towards equality practice depended on the efforts and enthusiasm of key individuals within schools. We now turn to evidence of practice within schools.

Policy into School Practice

Key People

At the school level, progress clearly depended on the degree of enthusiasm shown by the headteacher and senior management team as well as the support they received from the authority. In some places, it was reported, equal opportunities only featured on a school's agenda if there was a woman member of the senior management team. Given the rarity of women in such senior posts, the slow progress towards equality in some authorities was unsurprising. Research carried out in business and industrial organisations (Jewson, Drewett and Rossiter 1995) has also highlighted the importance of the capacity of senior women to stimulate action. Regional officials elsewhere confirmed this view:

> A major part of the problem of getting equal opportunities embedded in a school is to convince the headteacher.

> The attitude of the headteacher to equal opportunities (gender) is crucial in terms of what happens in a school.

The spokesperson from a rural authority (B) referred to the enthusiasm and "oomph" of the single female headteacher on an equal opportunities working group. Although other members were quite keen to complete the task she was seen to have provided the crucial impetus to carry things forward.

The common perception was that women tended to be much more active in promoting change than "white able-bodied men;" the latter, having benefited from the existing system, were regarded as feeling somewhat under threat, and "resisting change." Some older staff were said to be "dragging their feet" and one directorate official (Authority G, open door) suggested that the introduction of non-smoking and smoking areas in schools had proved more effective in bringing male and female teachers together than many exhortations and courses, because most schools could no longer provide separate staff rooms for men and women. (Scotland must be one of the last western countries to have retained such gendered staff accommodation).

Several authorities had undertaken positive action to redress the current imbalance in the distribution of senior management posts by providing "Women into Management" courses. Authority J (open door, positive action), for instance, offered such courses as well as "assertiveness training" for female staff, but in Authority G (open door) the practice of running separate courses had been abandoned because of complaints from male staff. Management courses were now targeted at all staff and organisers aimed for an equal gender balance on each one, which was usually achieved. An official from Authority C (structural transformation) reported that similar single-sex courses had caused "an awful lot of fuss from males" who took "a lot of convincing" about their legality and, it was further reported, women teachers who had attended the courses had experienced a backlash from older male colleagues on their return to school. So the authority introduced management courses for men as well.

In larger authorities each secondary school was expected to have a nominated person to take responsibility for equal opportunities. This post might be filled by the same person who had been the school's TVEI co-ordinator. Often the job of equal opportunities co-ordinator was undertaken by someone at the senior-teacher level but with very little time allocated for the task. The degree of enthusiasm with which these individuals tackled the job inevitably varied across schools.

Emphasis on Secondary Schools

Education authorities clearly recognised the importance of what happened at the individual school level. By providing in-service courses, advisory support, and various kinds of monitoring and audit procedures, they were seeking to bring the practice in all schools up to that operating in the best. However, spokespersons readily acknowledged that practice tended to lag behind published guidelines, or that it was inconsistent. Schools were said to exhibit a range of practice, from barely paying lip service to equal opportunities to a "dynamic, committed across-the-board" approach. It was clear, however, that far more progress had been made in the secondary than in the primary and special sectors; the latter sectors claimed much more frequently to adopt a child-centred approach.

The tendency for most authorities' developments in gender equality to concentrate in the secondary sector can be credited in large part to their involvement in TVEI. As respondents suggested, "I don't think they [primary schools] have done anything. It's not an issue. At the moment it's a TVEI equal opportunities policy but we would expect to spread it across all other age groups. But not yet." Another stated, "We don't have the resources to support the people in primary schools. Secondary schools can get cover paid for by TVEI."

Some authorities with larger populations had specifically included primary schools in their equal opportunities policies and developments, along with other parts of the education system, such as the careers service, psychological services, and community and nursery education. Furthermore, in some rural areas, primary and secondary pupils attended the same schools and so were subject to the same influences. Nevertheless, it is true to say that there has been much less progress in primary schools than in the secondary sector. Special schools, whether primary or secondary, were scarcely mentioned by our respondents. Despite this disparity among the sectors, a substantial number of statements were made which clearly indicated a growing realisation that the start of secondary education was really too late to begin raising pupils' awareness of gender-equality issues if attitudes prevalent in many communities were to be countered.

In many education authorities the secondary schools were expected to develop their own equal opportunities policies based on the authority's policy statement, and were encouraged to include equal opportunities in their school development plans. The leader of the Equality Education Team in one of the larger central belt authorities (C, structural transformation) reported the following as part of its plan: "To assist educational establishments and other agencies to develop and implement the authority's policy on multicultural and anti-racist education and equal opportunities."

However, several years of equal opportunities gender-development work across Scotland, despite being led and financed by TVEI, seemed to have had only limited impact on gender imbalance in relation to course choices, student destinations, and work-experience placements (though work-shadowing placements for senior pupils were frequently less traditional). Lack of progress on these issues was not blamed on schools and authorities alone. Employers were often reported to have entrenched views. Education was seen to be working in the context of a sexist society. As Gerver and Hart (1991) noted, the pattern in Scotland of low levels of female employment at the higher reaches of government, the civil service, law and business, as well as education, is "a more extreme variant of a common pattern elsewhere in the United Kingdom and in other European countries" (p. 20).

There were, and are, demonstrably fewer Scottish women in positions of power and influence than in comparable countries, so there have been relatively few role models for girls to follow. A directorate official from Education Authority D (positive action) remarked, "In Scotland we have no female judge, no female chief constable, only two women directors of education, only one director of social work, as I recall. Those may be hailed as signs of advance — but in themselves they define how much further we have to travel."

This feeling was well expressed by a spokesperson from Education Authority A (laissez faire) who suggested that, despite considerable effort having been made: "overall, outcomes have been poor." The spokesperson for Authority B (open door) explained it thus: "I am not in the business of changing hearts and minds." This was seen as too large a task to tackle. Rather, he sought to change people's behaviour, as a first step.

Positive Action

One relatively common aspect of practice was the initiation of various kinds of positive action, for both pupils and for staff, even in authorities whose policy statements placed them to the left of this position on the continuum. Much of this type of activity was instigated by TVEI. Positive action for pupils seemed to have been seen mainly in the limited terms of encouraging girls to make inroads into traditionally male areas. Activities included management courses for senior female pupils; assertiveness courses for pupils — especially girls; "girls into science and technology" days and courses; visits by the Women Into Science and Engineering (WISE) bus; and careers events with nonstereotypical role models.

Relatively little effort seemed to have been made in the opposite direction, however. Where were the parenting courses for boys? Were they being encouraged to consider female-dominated employment areas, such as primary teaching, the caring professions, foreign languages or office and business education? Did anyone tell them that men who do choose such professions often experience rapid promotion — "the glass escalator"? (Williams 1992).

Most "positive-action" activities were organised by the education authorities, often in conjunction with TVEI. Relatively little evidence was reported of positive action occurring at the level of the individual school. We heard of a handful of schools in Education Authority C, (structural transformation) which had run separate physics classes for girls during the first six weeks of an academic session to "get them over the hurdle." However, despite what the spokesperson referred to as "loads of research evidence" that this was an excellent way of helping girls into a traditional male subject, it was not a solution taken up widely. Successful experiments with single-sex technology classes and "boys-only" classes in Office and Information Studies in Region G (open door) were also reported.

Careers staff pointed to the impoverished reasons given by pupils for choosing (or not) a subject to study at standard or higher grade in the

Scottish Certificate of Education: "I don't like the teacher;" "My friend is doing it;" "It's a boys' subject;" "It's a girls' subject;" "My Mum/Dad thinks I should do it."

Despite teachers' efforts to imbue a wider sense of opportunity among these young people, their limited success suggested to them that parental pressure remained an important influence and parents "maybe have more stereotypical images and more limited experience." However, pupils' earlier school experience was also held to be important in affecting choices. Schools have a responsibility for promoting examination subjects in a non-biased way.

Indications of change were apparent in places. For example, in Authority K (structural transformation), although positive action was still seen mainly in terms of doing things to help girls change, the focus had moved from academic achievement (in which girls now outperformed boys) to the promotion of self-esteem (which was perceived as very low amongst a majority of girls). Some unease was expressed, however, about all the emphasis remaining on action to enhance the position of women and the aspirations of girls. Both girls and boys were expected to benefit from positive action and concern was expressed by some educators and parents about the low achievement of many boys and their apparent alienation from school. Several respondents indicated that it appeared easier for girls to move into non-stereotypical areas than for boys.

Overall Progress

Case studies of ten schools in three education authorities (five secondary, four primary, and one primary/secondary special) led us to conclude that progress towards gender equality in Scottish schools was generally limited. Even in authorities where the policy stance could be characterised as "structural transformation" only a minority of schools had fully embraced such a position. Elsewhere, we continued the process of "monitoring bleakness" (Brown 1993). Prerequisites for progress appeared to include:

1.   Grassroots pressure from classroom teachers. This is most likely to be found in urban areas where a "critical mass" of individuals could more easily form;
2.   A policy commitment from the top, preferably from both the individual institution and the authority;
3.   The presence of at least one key committed individual.

On the whole, gender equality in Scotland lagged behind that in comparable European Union countries. Even where the policy rhetoric at authority level placed it at the positive-action side of the continuum, there were few mechanisms to ensure that all institutions and individuals within that authority would be operating at that level.

Discussion

One of the problems associated with analysing the theoretical bases of policies and practices is the inevitably hybrid nature of the implicit theories. As we have argued elsewhere (Riddell 1992), although it is important to identify the underlying assumptions and goals of different policies, in practice many feminists hold in tension aspects of radical, socialist and liberal perspectives and this is reflected in school policies and classroom activities. Such tension is also evident in regional and national policies.

In an area like education, it can be argued that it is necessary to find some sort of compromise between, on the one hand, radical and socialist anti-sexist feminism and, on the other hand, liberal or bourgeois equal-opportunities approaches. If the oppression of women, and their exclusion (almost) from high-level decision making, are to be made explicit and challenged, then it is clear that anti-sexist perspectives are necessary to raise awareness of exploitation, whether the origin of that exploitation is seen as traditional patriarchy or as capitalism. Anti-sexist approaches, however, are fundamentally unsuited to providing solutions to immediate problems or bringing about short-term changes in practical situations. Their demands for equality of outcome assert the need for long-term struggles against systems. In contrast, liberal feminism emphasises equality of access and assumes that discrimination arises from outdated prejudice, which is amenable to change through rational argument. For schoolteachers and officers of educational policy-making bodies, all of whom have a responsibility for improving conditions for this generation of pupils, the liberal approach must appear a more fruitful path to follow for immediate solutions to gender problems. Furthermore, it feeds an accountability system which is essentially a checklist to demonstrate that, regardless of gender, equal opportunities are provided (and never mind whether equal outcomes are achieved?).

Both anti-sexist and liberal equal opportunity perspectives were evident in this study of Scottish schooling policies and practices. Within the policy statements of the main teachers' union (EIS), and to some extent those of the General Teaching Council, there were challenges to, and positive assertions of action against, sexism. The concern with questioning the assumptions and self-images of both boys and girls, and the firm rejection of approaches which regard girls as deficient boys who must be changed to fit with the priorities of a male curriculum, were features of a relatively radical stance. On the spectrum of education authority policies, the perspective of those at the positive-action/structural-transformation end was focused on working for equality of outcomes, not merely of access. As one respondent put it, the aim for employment was to have the same proportion of women in senior management positions as in the general workforce. But such anti-sexist strategies tend to arouse both hostility and ridicule from those who have no commitment to such a cause and resent being directed to behave in new ways. This was manifest in the male backlash against positive action through tailored training for women. Authorities which had something less than a firm commitment to radical ideas tended to abandon such action.

In stark contrast to the EIS and GTC policies, central government (SOEID) had taken only the weakest of liberal approaches. Although it was starting to include brief mentions of gender issues in curriculum guidance, the absence of a specific equal opportunities policy statement and the almost total neglect of gender matters in school inspections (the primary element in school accountability) provided evidence of a laissez-faire approach which emphasised individual choice (pupil, parent, employer) far more than social justice. Assertions by officials that it was not for central government to direct authorities or schools on this aspect of education rang hollow in a context where "guidance" statements on such matters as what to teach, how to teach it, and how to group pupils were legion.

The evidence on practice in schools suggested that in only a small minority of cases (all of these were in education authorities which approached a structural-transformation stance) was there any challenge on fundamental issues such as the domestic division of labour, the career structure of teaching, the sexual politics of the school and workplace, or the nature of the curriculum. Much more common was a liberal approach which encouraged women to improve their skills and attitudes, with special urging of girls to study science and technology (but with no questioning of the privileged status accorded to these curricular areas in western culture). The economic arguments for development in this area were given an equal opportunities slant whereby girls must be offered the same choices as boys in the employment markets and the pathways to promotion, and the same opportunities to fulfil the government's labour requirements. A more equitable approach, within a liberal framework, would be to use positive action strategies to encourage and then support boys who wish to move into non-traditional areas.

The great advantage of the liberal approach is that it provides something for the individual practitioner to do. It is not necessary to wait for a revolution to transform the whole system before taking action which will bring some satisfaction. The question to be addressed, however, is whether the liberal strategy of accepting the status quo, encouraging girls and women into traditionally male areas, believing that the system can be changed through individual effort, and assuming that sex inequality is not inevitable, will (1) remedy social injustice or (2) simply reinforce an unjust state of affairs by tweaking it to make it appear less discriminatory. Data from some of the primary schools in this study illustrated the latter alternative: emphasis on meeting the needs of individual children had the effect of reinforcing many of the gender-discriminatory ideas and practices which children had developed before schooling began or continued to experience in their local community.

Maclean (1994) has distinguished an individual equal opportunities approach in Scotland, which seeks to provide the conditions for young people to rise through the system by ability and hard work, from a collectivist or anti-sexist stance, which concentrates on identifying and transforming social structures impeding the development of groups rather than individuals. She has described the manifestation of both approaches in gender equality work in education as a "seemingly paradoxical co-existence" of individualism and collectivism arising out of a culture of poverty. As Paterson (1983, p. 198) explained, "in conditions of severe scarcity, winning a share of the few rewards available produces both competition and co-operation."

Maclean maintained that it is important to identify whether school-based gender equality work may be identified as individualist or collectivist. The fact that we find both in Scottish schools may be an indicator of the impoverished state of this aspect of social justice in our education system. In some, though not all, education authority areas, frail gender equality measures suffered from stated commitments to individualism. Such individualism is inevitably fragmented, is sustained by a general reluctance to challenge what appear to be child-centred concerns, and does virtually nothing to change discriminatory attitudes and practices in the community. There is resistance to more radical approaches, which are regarded as harsh collectivism. This is compounded by widespread failure to evaluate the outcomes of the modest efforts which are in place. As Jewson, Mason, Drewett and Rossiter (1995) comment, monitoring ensures that patterns of group disadvantage remain visible even in a situation where equal opportunities policy is increasingly focused on individuals.

While it is accepted that a practical liberal approach to gender issues characterises most activity in Scottish schools, there are considerable dangers of seeing this strategy as appropriate for the future rather than as a bare minimum requirement for the present. Without the addition of a more radical, collectivist lead from central government and those education authorities which currently do little more than fulfil the legal requirements, gains made on the gender equality front are likely to atrophy and relationships between groups deteriorate. It is clear that changes in thinking about these matters take time, but teachers and others engaged in the education of young people of school age have a responsibility to reflect in new ways on the gender discrimination which still pervades the education system. Grass-roots initiatives are essential, but so is an external "push" from the policy-making edifice. The aim has to be for a more purposeful and interdependent collaboration. It may be the case that in such a collaborative enterprise the provision of special arrangements to counteract collective gender disadvantage can result in the longer term in a more equal educational world in which the focus for positive action will be on "individuals and their self-realisation rather than on groups and distributive justice" (Jewson, Mason, Drewett and Rossiter 1995, p. iii).

In a minority of authorities and schools we found that already there was an impressive determination to establish equal opportunities practice. Acceptance of responsibility in this area was readily evident among senior managers who saw the importance of combining leadership and standard-setting with efforts to help practitioners reflect on and question their own attitudes towards gender equality. The discomforts which come with monitoring, challenging and regulating people's ways of working were seen as inevitable steps in the journey towards achievement of an educational culture which abhors discrimination. That journey would be substantially eased if central government were to exert more explicit legal and moral pressure.

Notes

1. The work reported here formed part of the research funded by the Equal Opportunities Commission (EOC) on the impact of recent educational reforms on gender equality in Scottish schools (Turner et al. 1995). Versions of figures 1–3 appeared in that publication and we are grateful to the EOC for permission to reproduce them here. However, the views reported in this chapter are those of the authors and not of the EOC.

References

Acker, S. 1994. Feminist theory and the study of gender and education. In S. Acker, ed., *Gendered Education*. Buckingham: Open University Press, 43–54.

Brown, S.A. 1993. Research on gender in education: Monitoring bleakness or instigating change. *Scottish Affairs* 5: 107–17.

Educational Institute of Scotland. 1989. Report of ad hoc committee on anti-sexist policy, Minute No 559 of Annual General Meeting. Edinburgh: EIS.

Educational Institute of Scotland. 1990a. *Sexism and You*. Edinburgh: EIS.

Educational Institute of Scotland. 1990b. *Sexism and Institutions*. Edinburgh: EIS.

Educational Institute of Scotland. 1996. *EIS Anti-Sexist Policy Update: Parts 1 & 2*. Edinburgh: EIS.

Eisenstein, H. 1984. *Contemporary Feminist Thought*. London: Unwin.

Equal Opportunities Commission (EOC). 1995. *Equal Opportunities in Education And Training in Scotland: Setting the Agenda*. Glasgow: EOC.

Farish, M., J. McPake, J. Powney, and G. Weiner,. 1995. *Equal Opportunities in Colleges and Universities*. Buckingham: The Society for Research into Higher Education and Open University Press.

Fewell, J. & F.M.S. Paterson. 1990. *Girls in Their Prime: Scottish Education Revisited*. Edinburgh: Scottish Academic Press.

General Teaching Council for Scotland. 1991. *Gender in Education: A GTC Policy Document*. Edinburgh: GTC.

Gerver, E., and L. Hart. 1991. *Strategic Women: How Do They Manage In Scotland?* Aberdeen: Aberdeen University Press

Hills, L. 1990. 'The Senga syndrome: Reflections on 21 years in education. In J. Fewell, and F.M.S. Paterson, eds., *Girls in Their Prime: Scottish Education Revisited*. Edinburgh: Scottish Academic Press.

Jewson, N., D. Mason, A. Drewett, and W. Rossiter. 1995. *Formal Equal Opportunities Policies and Employment Best Practice*. Sheffield: Department of Employment, Research Series.

Macintosh, M. 1993. The gender imbalance in Scottish education. *Scottish Affairs* 5: 118–23.

Maclean, C. 1994. The theory and practice of equal opportunities in Scotland. *Scottish Affairs* 6: 36–51.

Paterson, H. 1983. Incubus and ideology: The development of secondary schooling in Scotland, 1900-1939. In W.M. Humes and H.M. Paterson, eds., *Scottish Future and Scottish Education*. Edinburgh: John Donald.

Riddell, S. 1992. 'Gender and education: Progressive and conservative forces in the balance. In S. Brown and S. Riddell, eds., *Race, Class and Gender in Schools*. Edinburgh: SCRE, 44–53.

46   *Gender Issues in International Education:Beyond Policy*

Scottish Consultative Council on the Curriculum. 1993. *Curriculum and Assessment 5–14: Cross Curricular Aspects.* Dundee: SCCC.
Scottish Consultative Council on the Curriculum. nd, a. *Equal Opportunities: A statement of position.* Dundee: SCCC.
Scottish Consultative Council on the Curriculum. nd, b. *Equal Opportunities in Practice,* Dundee: SCCC.
Scottish Examinations Board. 1995. Gender and SCE Examinations. *SEB Research 3.* Dalkeith: SEB.
Scottish Office Education Department. 1991a. *Curriculum and Assessment in Scotland: National Guidelines: English Language.* Edinburgh: HMSO.
Scottish Office Education Department. 1991b. *Curriculum and Assessment in Scotland: National Guidelines: Mathematics.* Edinburgh: HMSO.
Scottish Office Education Department. 1992. *Curriculum and Assessment in Scotland: National Guidelines: Reporting 5–14: Promoting Partnership.* Edinburgh: HMSO.
Turner, E., S. Riddell, and S. Brown. 1995. *Gender Equality in Scottish Schools: The Impact of Recent Educational Reforms.* Manchester: Equal Opportunities Commission.
Williams, C.L. 1992. The glass escalator: hidden advantages for men in the female professions. *Social Problems* 39(3): August, 253–67.

Appendix 1

Education Authorities have been randomly assigned an identifying letter. These are listed with a brief description of regional characteristics (where small/medium/large is used it refers to population size — under 250,000; 250,000–500,000; over 500,000).

Scottish Education Authorities (1995)

Authority	Description
A	small population, rural environment
B	small population, rural environment
C	large population, predominantly urban, central belt
D	medium population, predominantly rural, some large towns
E	small Islands Authority
F	small Islands Authority
G	small population, rural environment
H	medium population, mixed rural/urban, no large towns
I	small Islands Authority
J	large population, predominantly rural, one major town
K	large population, predominantly urban with substantial rural areas
L	medium population, mixed rural urban, several small towns

CHAPTER 3

Equal Opportunity Initiatives: England, Wales and the Netherlands Compared

Maggie Wilson and Hetty Dekkers

In common with other European countries, there has been a massive influx of women workers into the paid labour forces of the Netherlands and England and Wales beginning in the 1960s, and gaining momentum during the 1980s. However, in all European countries this growth in women's employment has been characterised by a parallel deepening of divisions within the labour force, where female employees are experiencing increasing inequalities in pay, unemployment rates, and job security (Plantenga 1995). Eighty-two percent of part-time jobs in Europe were occupied by women in 1991 and much of this work is governed by irregular hours, low pro-rata wages, low status, and a lack of promotion opportunities or long-term prospects, made more complicated by child-care provision that is inadequate to meet the needs of many working parents (EC Network on Childcare 1996).

In the Netherlands, the percentage of women in the labour force rose by 12 percent between 1981 and 1994, to constitute 42 percent of the labour force. This increase has been particularly due to the entry of highly educated women between the ages of 25 and 45 into the labour market and to an increase in the number of working women with children under 18 years old. Thirty-three percent of Dutch women worked part-time in 1994, as compared with 10 percent of men. The wage differential between men and women working more than 20 hours per week was about 20 percent in 1994 for reasons of their labour market position and level (Ministry of Social Affairs and Employment 1995).

Labour force statistics are usually given for the United Kingdom as a whole, rather than the specific focus of the chapter on the education system of England and Wales. In the United Kingdom, similar patterns are to be observed, although it has the second highest female economic participation rate, after Denmark. By 2006 it is estimated that women will constitute 48 percent of the labour force (*Social Trends* 1995). About 45 percent of all women work part-time. This group earns about 60 percent of the male hourly average rate and 75 percent of the female full-time rate (*Social Trends* 1995). Despite some incursions into traditional male areas of work, many jobs remain sex-specific. Although there have been some changes in the traditional division of labour within the home, in both countries women still undertake the major share of domestic work, whether or not they are in paid employment. In both countries there is a particularly low level of state-funded day care for children, especially for children under three (Pot 1995).

As in other European countries, there has been a rapid and sometimes remarkable progress in the improvement of girls' educational opportunities in terms of enrolment and access to institutions since the 1970s. Although entry into higher education should be treated as a limited benchmark among many, it is nonetheless significant that in the Netherlands the proportion of women completing university rose from 18 percent in 1975 to almost 50 percent in 1996, while the number of women students in full-time higher education in the U.K. rose from 41 percent in 1979–80 to 50 percent in 1994–5 (DfEE 1996). Yet despite the considerable progress made, stubborn and persistent divisions remain within education as they do in the labour market (Wilson 1990; Dekkers 1994).

In both the Netherlands and in England and Wales concerted attempts to redress inequalities in education have been made since the mid-1970s, with varying degrees of success. Although influenced to a large degree by the different political structure and style of the two systems, each provides a different model of policy development and implementation and throws issues of mutual importance into relief.

Equal Opportunities Policies in the Netherlands

The Process of Policy Formation

In order to understand the role of the state in equal opportunities initiatives, it is important to clarify the extent to which the Dutch government can exercise influence over the curriculum and internal organisation of Dutch schools. The education system is divided (or "pillarised") along religious lines, each school falling within the state,

Catholic, Protestant, or non-denominational private sectors. State schools are run by either local or central government. The private sector, which constitutes a very small part of educational provision, caters to religious minorities or acts as a support to schools run on particular pedagogical principles, such as Montessori schools. All schools are co-educational.

Since 1917 the Dutch constitution has ensured that the state supports schools financially in all four sectors, yet all schools are free to arrange their own education, provided that certain basic requirements are met. State control is thus limited, although the state can recommend general policy initiatives (Arends and Volman 1992). The Dutch national curriculum comprises a broad framework of principles and directives and lacks the very detailed prescription of the current national curriculum for England and Wales. As in the U.K., education is compulsory between the ages of 5 and 16, but there is no system of comprehensive secondary education at present. At the age of 12 children are directed into one of three different levels within the sphere of general advanced secondary education or into vocational education, on the basis of testing and informal assessment. There is a tendency for more girls than boys to be directed into general advanced education and within each sphere, familiar patterns of gender differentiation in terms of subject uptake are apparent, despite significant changes during the 1970s and 1980s.

Since the early 1970s equal opportunity (gender) has been an important component of Dutch governmental policy, strengthening principles already enshrined in the Dutch constitution. The feminist movement of the late 1960s and the 1975 United Nations International Women's Year created pressure which could not be ignored by the social democratic government of the time. In 1974 the government founded the Equal Opportunities Committee (later renamed the Equal Opportunities Council), an advisory body with a remit to design and implement equal opportunity policies, and the issue was also explicitly added to the Ministry of Cultural, Recreational and Social Affairs. Since then, one cabinet minister has been charged with the responsibility of matters pertaining to equal opportunities and there has been a general policy of integrating equal opportunities objectives in all legislative areas (the so-called facet policy).

The Ministry of Education and Science published three policy documents between 1979 and 1985. The first contained 92 policy measures, with the aims of

- reducing the factors which delimit subject and occupational choice;

- re-evaluating traditionally feminine qualities;
- redressing the imbalance of recruitment of girls and boys in subject areas.

The 1980 document focussed largely on study choices and critically reviewed the way in which many initiatives taken had been marginal to mainstream education and had tended not to emphasise the involvement of boys in non-traditional areas of study (Arends and Volman 1992). By 1985, with a general trend away from specific policy measures to an integrated approach, the emphasis shifted again to incorporating educational policy into general equal opportunities policies for all ministries, alongside some specific projects. The 1985 document did address the issues of school organisation and gender differentiation at primary school level, but during the late 1980s the focus swung back to examining study choices and the under-representation of girls in certain subject areas at secondary school level.

In the wider sphere of social and economic policy there has been a gradual acceptance that the increasing participation of women in the labour market is not sufficient in itself to guarantee emancipation. The Strategy Programme for Equal Opportunities 1987–1990 defined the keynotes of policy as the elimination of gender-stereotyped behaviour and the achievement of structural change, in conjunction with new initiatives in positive action on the shop floor and the encouragement of more women to enter entrepreneurial activities and traditionally male occupational spheres. In the latest equal opportunities programme, "With a View to 1995," published by the Ministry of Social Services and Employment, labour participation features as a main issue. The programme contains general and specific ministerial objectives in improving the economic independence of women. Initially, only general policy statements were concerned with the "redistribution of unpaid labour," defined as the promotion of traditionally feminine and domestic skills among boys and men, with no specific policy measures outlined. Indeed, this objective was only added at the very last minute to the 1993 Equal Opportunities in Education Memorandum published by the Ministry of Education and Science, due to pressure from women's organisations. The Memorandum also broadened the range of policy objectives to include the position of women teachers and educational managers, the education of immigrant girls and the sociocultural independence of girls.

The rationale behind such policy has been criticised by various sections of the women's movement. It is argued that the later focus on economic self-sufficiency ignores the existing division of labour between the sexes, which tends to influence choices in education incompatible with stated governmental objectives. National policy is said to have been led more by labour market demands than by inherent equal opportunity objectives, and tends to "blame the victim" for "wrong" or inappropriate study and career choices. In the long term, change could be effected by counteracting stereotyped attitudes at primary school level, which could result in wider opportunities for economic independence at a later stage. However, such long-term objectives could leave girls "high and dry," if not supported by the provision of appropriate technical and vocational skills. In addition, the gradual withdrawal from the 1979 objective of the re-evaluation of feminine and masculine attributes and skills cannot support the broadest objectives of government policy. These contradictory strands of policy, it is argued, represent a dualism within state policy. The liberal aim of promoting equal opportunities within an unequal system sits unhappily with the more radical proposed re-evaluation of masculine and feminine potential within Dutch society.

In terms of the policy process, the transition from a specific to an integrated policy approach in 1985 seems to have created a gap and has led to a virtual standstill in implementation and diffusion of objectives. Not only do the structural limitations created by the state's lack of influence on the private and denominational sectors create a gap between theory and practice, but the government appears to be relinquishing equal opportunity initiatives to individual schools and teachers in all sectors. At present there is no planned implementation strategy, but it is assumed that initiatives will have a cascade effect in local schools. As many of the policy objectives are lofty and present few implementation guidelines, the translation of policy into practice has been reliant on ad hoc initiatives.

The Scope and Character of Equal Opportunities Initiatives in the Netherlands

As outlined in the previous section, equal opportunity initiatives in the Netherlands have increasingly emphasised occupational qualifications and, in particular, have encouraged girls to choose scientific and technical subjects in both academic and vocational education. There have been no published initiatives in pre-school education and limited work in primary schools. The main initiative here was a mid-1980's National Institute for Curriculum Development programme which focussed on screening books and developing teaching materials aimed at changing attitudes towards sex roles.

Early national projects in secondary schools were concerned with promoting "freedom of choice" in school options and employment. Schools were encouraged to promote a general change of mentality towards the position of women in society, through the provision of time off classroom duties for teachers. However, projects brought about little change in study choices and few tangible results and, in line with policy recommendations, initiatives became more directly aimed at getting girls to take scientific subjects, despite the uneven participation of boys in other areas of the curriculum, such as languages.

The most well-known campaign was entitled "Choose Science" and ran from 1986 to 1989. This promoted an awareness of the importance of science through school-based activities (films, leaflets, etc.) and through the media. Opposition to the campaign came not only from languages and humanities teachers, who feared job losses, but also from mathematics teachers, who were unwilling to teach "weaker" pupils. In fact, the campaign did not result in any significant quantitative results, and was followed by a more neutral and broadly based campaign, entitled "A Smart Girl Is Ready for the Future." This stressed a wider understanding of the independence of girls, and was more favourably received by schools.

In addition, school-based activities, with or without government funding, have been concerned with the provision of "gender friendly" teaching materials in the sciences. There has been little systematic evaluation of such initiatives and therefore little is known of their effectiveness, despite reported teacher enthusiasm.

Careers counsellors have also been involved at this level. Professional journals have encouraged counsellors not only to draw pupils' attention to government-produced materials, but also to stress positive action in options guidance and in personal interviews, particularly when evaluating pupils' examination results. However, the other side of the coin is also regularly mentioned: objections are raised against recruiting girls into science and technology "at any cost."

In vocational education, initiatives have been directed at encouraging girls away from courses leading to the caring professions and at boosting their interest in technology. This has been introduced as a compulsory subject in basic vocational education and there is support for introducing it in primary schools. Publicity campaigns have been run by the state to recruit girls on to technical courses and the Equal Opportunities Office for Vocational Education subsidises projects aimed at increasing and retaining girls' participation in junior secondary technical education. In general, although many schools take up such publicity and information campaigns, their effects, in terms of changed patterns of recruitment, are very small (Dekkers 1996).

State-sponsored projects concerning girls from minority groups ran from 1986 to 1989, with follow-up projects in 1991. The main focus of these projects was not whether girls are receiving technical education, but whether these projects were preventing absenteeism, discouraging girls from leaving school without formal qualifications and encouraging them to transfer to higher forms of education. Initial evaluation has suggested that such projects are more successful in acting as support groups than in changing achievement levels (Dekkers, van Lieshout and Stortelder 1989). The new so-called pilot projects (from 1995) are according to more positive recent research, aimed at support and counselling within mainstream education.

The Ministry of Education and Science also set up an Equal Opportunities in Management Office in 1994 to co-ordinate policy aimed at improving the position of female pupils and staff in vocational education, particularly on short senior-level courses and in part-time nonformal education.

In higher education, initiatives have largely concerned the recruitment of girls into the three Dutch technical universities. Since 1982 these initiatives have included open-house days for upper secondary schoolgirls, with the aim of introducing them to and interesting them in technology and technical professions. This campaign has now been formally evaluated and the resultant changes in patterns of choice appear to be minimal (Dekkers 1990). The root of the problem lies in the fact that by the end of secondary education, study choices are already pre-empted by earlier choices and qualifications: therefore a sufficient pool of potential recruits will not exist to any great extent, unless measures are taken at an earlier stage. Initiatives to monitor the performance of girls who have opted for higher technical education have, however, been successful in encouraging student retention in male-dominated subject areas.

In general, initiatives have been carried out by a few enthusiastic and committed teachers and have therefore not been systematically evaluated. The government has offered free and voluntary in-service training to teachers but participation has been very low. Negative reaction by the media, parents and teachers to the more radical dimensions of earlier policy has been succeeded by some support for liberal initiatives or, at worst, by apathy. Criticism of the narrowness of the science and technology recruitment campaigns has been widespread.

In recent years, continuous pressure by women's lobbying groups at the national level has resulted in the inclusion of home economics and health care as a compulsory component of the lower secondary curriculum. Whether this will be presented as a chance to promote

attitudinal change among boys or as a purely academic subject remains
to be seen. The inclusion of "care-independency" (social independence
and the ability to take on caring roles) for boys as a major policy
objective of the 1993 policy memorandum can likewise be seen as a
significant departure from earlier campaigns. A central office, set up to
give shape to equal opportunities in the lower secondary national core
curriculum, has been mandated responsibility for making the concept of
"care-independency" practicable in the education system. So far the
concept of re-evaluating traditional women's occupations and unpaid
work has met with little political support. Indeed, there is some evidence
of a shift away from the impetus to "reappraise the feminine" towards a
renewed focus on girls' attitudes as the root of the problem (Volman, van
Eck, and ten Dam 1995).

Equal Opportunities Policies in England and Wales

The Process of Policy Formation

In contrast with the Netherlands, England and Wales have provided little
central-state direction in the area of equal opportunities in England and
Wales. There have been no central state committees of inquiry, no
central state funds devoted specifically to promoting equal opportunities
in education and no explicit policy statements from the Department for
Education and Employment on the subject (Arnot, David, and Weiner
1996). Rather, the DfEE has tended to shift responsibility on to the Local
Education Authorities (LEAs) and to adopt a minimalist approach.
Although this has been described in one analysis of British policy as
"doing good by doing little" (Kirp, Yudof, and Franks 1987), others have
strongly criticised the absence of a central state commitment to this area
(Arnot 1987; Riley 1994). The impetus for the introduction of equal
opportunity policies has largely emanated from the LEAs, teacher
unions, teachers and more recently from the government-appointed
inspectorate.

    The lack of central direction by the DfEE is in marked contrast with
increasingly interventionist policies in the area of organisational and
curriculum reform since 1984. An increasing emphasis on educational
standards and performance from the late 1980s onwards was partly
fuelled by a critique of "progressive education" as responsible for the
economic ills of the country. Arguments for social justice ceded place to
arguments about resource maximisation. Under a radical Conservative
government, power has been shifted from the education professionals

and Local Education Authorities to central government. A decline in public expenditure on education, coupled with the introduction of market accountability through increased competition among schools, has resulted in a greatly changed educational climate (Riley 1994). Key initiatives in the late 1980s onwards included the introduction of a national curriculum in 1988; the restructuring of public examinations taken at 16+ in 1988; regular testing of pupils at the ages of 7, 11, and 14, and the publication of "league tables" of school examination results. Organisational changes included the diminution of local authority controls on schools and the devolution of budgets to school level.

Where the Dutch government guidelines give a very broad framework for the content of the curriculum, the recent process of curriculum reform in England and Wales has been elaborate and extensive, initially resulting in detailed prescription running to several volumes of documentation. Although the documentation was slimmed down in the early 1990s as a result of pressure from teachers and parents, it could still be argued that this has moved the education system, over the course of a few years, from a position of virtual autonomy in matters pertaining to the curriculum to one much nearer the models provided by the French system or former U.S.S.R. Yet, it is significant that equal opportunities were only identified in the national curriculum as a crosscurricular dimension, left to schools to work out in practice. The only major programme of action in education with a specific commitment to addressing gender imbalances has been provided by the Manpower Services Commission, under the aegis of the former Department of Employment. Here, the TVEI (Technical and Vocational Education Initiative) programme, which has provided substantial resources to develop a broad range of work in this area, includes a contractual requirement that schools should ensure that programmes encourage girls to take up non-traditional subject choices and that equal numbers of boys and girls take part in the programme. This is reinforced by the requirement that these aspects should be monitored and included in progress reports (Measor and Sikes 1992). Although the programme has not been entirely successful in fulfilling these aims, it does provide a model of political assertion, akin to the American concept of contract compliance, and has often been cited by teachers as a useful form of legitimation for equal opportunities work (Ruddock 1994).

In the wider arena of policy-making, years of lobbying resulted in the 1975 Sex Discrimination Act, which is still the one major focus of gender policy in England and Wales today. Despite the establishment of the Equal Opportunities Commission as a "watchdog" research organisation and arbitration facilitator, the Act provided limited

measures of legal redress against discrimination and was generally
concerned with the liberal goals of equality of access and opportunity,
rather than equality of outcome. It has provided a platform for
addressing institutional and curricular barriers to girls in education but
does not address the hidden curriculum or present such issues in a
broader socioeconomic context. Under the Conservative administration
from 1979 to 1997, there was little demonstrable commitment to gender
equality at the Cabinet level. In contrast to the Netherlands, the British
government issued no mandate to include gender issues in the remit of
different ministries and no minister was responsible for women's affairs
at this level. Indeed, statements by several leading politicians regarding
the traditional home-based place of women, and the government's
refusal to provide tax relief for childcare or adequate childcare facilities,
were illustrative of the position of the majority of those in power. The
new Labour government, elected in May 1997, has not appointed a
minister whose sole responsibility is gender policy. Instead this remit
has been added to the existing portfolio of the Social Services Minister
(who happens to be a woman). The change of government has raised
expectations of a change, but at the time of writing, it is not clear how
far these expectations will be realised.

The Sex Discrimination Act places a general "duty" on the Local
Education Authorities to guard against discrimination. This has been
interpreted variably within their local areas of jurisdiction . In the early
1980s, when there was a more balanced relationship between the central
state and local government, initiatives tended to be confined to the large
Labour-controlled metropolitan authorities, such as Leeds, Sheffield,
Manchester, and the Inner London Education Authority. The overt
commitment to radical anti-sexist measures apparent in such
programmes often provoked considerable local hostility among
councillors, orchestrated by the local press. One such programme in
Humberside received criticism ranging from being portrayed as
disruptive and a waste of public time and money to "silly," "paranoid"
and "sinister" (Headlam-Wells 1985). Such criticisms have to be seen in
the wider context of "moral panic" concerning the "left-wing invasion"
of schools in the tabloid press at that time. In the late 1980s initiatives
spread to a broader range of LEAs, including the rural "shire" counties,
such as Hertfordshire and Leicestershire. The majority of LEAs now
have an equal opportunities policy in force. Whilst they often served as
a smokescreen for inactivity, they also legitimated school-based
programmes and helped to release limited funds available for such work,
as several published accounts of initiatives testify. Many appointed
Equal Opportunities Advisors or Advisory Support Teachers. Several

invested in programmes designed to have a "cascade" effect, for example by giving staff time off classroom teaching to a designated teacher to take part in a working group drawn from local schools.

A number of examples of such LEA-based or sponsored projects were published in the 1980s, (e.g., Gibbs 1989; Trickett 1989; Cunnison and Gurevitch 1990). Such accounts tended to be descriptive, with some analysis of the process of policy implementation. In most cases, formal evaluation of programmes was carried out, often conducted by independent university-based researchers. High-profile programmes appeared to be relatively successful in creating a general awareness of and support for equal opportunities among teachers. Much of this success was dependent on securing financial support and staff release from the LEA, the moral and political support of senior school management and on acting in a consortium of schools, to combat teacher isolation.

In the 1990s the reduced role of LEAs has resulted in less high-profile work. Most LEA involvement is now concerned with providing a monitoring service of staffing patterns and pupil performance, providing in-service education for teachers and governors and helping schools to prepare for inspection.

Since 1993, regular government inspection of schools has required the provision of information on equal opportunities policies in the areas of access, student enrolment, and staffing. This has been seen as largely beneficial in raising the profile of equal opportunities in schools, even if questions of classroom management and the hidden curriculum are not included (Arnot, David, and Weiner 1996).

The Scope and Character of Equal Opportunities Initiatives in England and Wales

What published accounts of equal opportunities initiatives do not tend to stress is the way in which gender issues are presented. As work in this area spread throughout the 1980s, so the radical cutting edge of many of the earlier projects was dulled. With some notable exceptions, such as the Inner London Education Authority's strong anti-sexist stance, the emphasis came to be placed far more on the liberal concern of equality of opportunity within a competitive arena, with some scope for positive action. Equal opportunities became identified as good educational practice and so began to be represented on mainstream agendas. As one male headteacher in Sheffield is reported as saying: "I think there are a lot of people who are genuinely committed to a good education for kids and see equal opportunities, particularly in the gender area, as being crucial to our kids" (Agnew et al. 1989, p. 41).

High-profile national projects also tended to be associated with unlocking the door to wider opportunities for girls and young women, especially in the areas of science and technology. This new emphasis on vocationalism in education, combined with the equal opportunity lobby, has been described as an unusual marriage (Weiner 1989). GATE (Girls and Technology Education), WISE (Women Into Science and Engineering), and GIST (Girls Into Science and Technology) offered a new stimulus for change in the 1980s. Backed up by sufficient resources of time and expertise, they contributed to the establishment of equal opportunities as a legitimate area of debate and activity. GIST, in particular, benefited from a rigorous evaluation strategy, comprising a variety of observational and survey-based techniques (Whyte 1985). Although results were mixed in terms of both attitudinal change and changes in patterns of subject uptake, the project gained a high national profile, attempted to produce the kinds of quantitative data now much in vogue in central government circles and also deployed imaginative implementation strategies, such as the GIST roadshows. WISE was aimed at all levels of education, not just upper secondary pupils, but was more narrowly focussed on the effects of the masculine image of science and engineering on female pupils. It is significant that equal opportunities were presented as good mainstream practice and involved substantial teacher input in research and implementation, an exercise in "top-down" change designed to have a "bottom-up" ripple effect.

The campaigns had a limited effect on student enrolment, concentrating as they did on the image of science and technology rather than the experiences of women in scientific and technological employment (Hernwood 1996). They were, however, arguably the kind of project which the then Department for Education and Science should have sponsored, rather than leaving the sponsorship of such initiatives to such bodies as the Equal Opportunities Commission, the Engineering Council, or private industry. This emphasis compares with the dominant theme in Dutch campaigns of the same decade, notably the "Choose Science" campaign, sponsored by the Dutch government. Although gaining a higher media profile, the Dutch example was perhaps less sophisticated in its implementation strategy, reminiscent of the biblical parable of the sower who went forth to sow, scattering seed at random, with very mixed results.

Early school-based initiatives in England and Wales were carried out by what Weiner has described as the "pioneering cohort" of dedicated feminists in schools and LEAs, many committed to a radical anti-sexist perspective (Weiner 1989). These initiatives were mostly concerned with the removal of sexist practices, increasing girls' confidence, and labour market considerations. Several studies have reflected entrenched teacher attitudes towards gender issues, with variation according to age, subject specialism, sex, and graduate status (Pratt, Bloomfield and Searle 1984; Kelly 1987; Thompson 1989). Kelly's study of "traditionalists and trendies" also included region as a variable, but the relationship between teachers' ideologies and chosen working area is probably a symbiotic one. One often-quoted study described the plight of many of the early pioneers in staffroom politics: "It is frightening how quickly we run into hostility or dismissive amusement even when quite small changes are suggested and facing such reactions can be a daunting prospect" (Ord and Quigley 1985, p. 100). This experience is echoed in several published reports, where teachers describe how they were made to feel marginal, silly, or worse (e.g., Trickett 1989; Ruddock 1994).

Initial and in-service teacher education appears to have lagged behind developments in schools. Despite recommendations by the Council for Teacher Accreditation in 1985 that equal opportunities should permeate initial teacher education, such issues are often presented unsystematically in single sessions, if at all, and do not permeate professional studies in many teacher education departments and institutions (Carr 1989; Skelton 1989; Thompson 1989; Sikes 1991). In the study by Sikes, 25 percent of the 185 "raw recruits" on the first year of an initial teacher-training course expected boys to be reckless, untidy, cheeky, brave, noisy and naughty, and girls to be tidy, clean, quick, sensible, obedient, passive and well-behaved. The majority expressed negative attitudes towards interpersonal discrimination but did not see this in terms of their own classroom practice, reflecting the "not in my backyard" mentality expressed by many established teachers (Pratt, Bloomfield, and Searle 1984).

Yet the early pioneers made a significant and rarely acknowledged contribution through a huge variety of often short-lived and usually underfunded initiatives in many primary and secondary schools, drawing support from lateral networks, such as Women in Education. The majority of these have not been documented in mainstream literature and have not been formally evaluated, perhaps partly for ideological reasons but also because the aims of such work were often radical, intangible and diffuse, involving broad consciousness-raising around such issues as sexuality and sexual harassment. It is at this level that attempts have been made to address the "re-evaluation of traditionally feminine qualities" or boys' "care-independency," which have been a theme in Dutch government documents. Rare examples of working with boys at primary and secondary levels are provided by

Askew and Ross (1988) and Reay (1990 and 1993), involving sensitive and imaginative strategies to explore masculine and feminine attributes in a supportive setting. The compulsory inclusion of what has been known as "home economics" or "domestic science" in the technology component of the national curriculum may help to enhance boys' "care-independency" in future years. For some time several primary schools have regarded this as an essential part of the knowledge base of all children.

A good example is provided by a Humberside school where visits were arranged by male caregivers, such as a male nurse, alongside visits by women in non-traditional occupations, such as a female car mechanic. Although no formal evaluation was made, it was reported that girls and boys responded with equal enthusiasm (Cunnison and Gurevitch 1990). However, where secondary schools have organised the technology curriculum along modular lines, with choice between components, there is some evidence to suggest that the old patterns are re-emerging. Additionally, more recent work has reflected how many of the "gender" initiatives of the 1980s left many boys and men in schools feeling confused, hostile, and defensive. Most work which has addressed changing notions of masculinity has either occurred in Personal and Social Education in secondary schools or through external youth work agencies (Jackson and Salisbury 1996). Working with boys also poses a dilemma for some feminists, as expressed by Reay: "How far should I be devoting my energy to boys, who already demand disproportionate amounts of teacher attention at the expense of girls?" (1993, p. 21).

Addressing issues of sexuality within the national curriculum is still reported to set alarm bells ringing, particularly after strident criticism by the "New Right" of such work in schools in the early 1990s (Redman 1994).

As in the Netherlands, there have been few published accounts of developments at infant or nursery school level in England and Wales. These appear to be limited to a few initiatives in metropolitan areas, where teachers have, for example, monitored children's choice of play activities or the use of language by teachers (Browne and France 1986; Trickett 1989).

A contrast is provided, however, by the development of whole school policies, especially at primary school level. As outlined earlier, there has been no systematic and structural basis to the Dutch programme (Arends and Volman 1992). Where a strong lead has been taken by LEAs in England and Wales, the development of whole school policies in some schools has had the advantage of bringing the issue of equal opportunities to the centre stage, involving school governing bodies and teachers and addressing both the curriculum and school organisation (Weiner 1990; Claire, Maybin, and Swann 1993). While primary schools often see this as an integral part of their work, secondary schools are more likely to have stated equal opportunities policies. The majority of these have been developed since 1989, in the wake of decreased LEA control. In a recently published survey, 50 percent of secondary schools reported having equal opportunities working groups or co-ordinators, but the majority of schools defined such issues as "one of a number" and secondary to other priorities (Arnot, David, and Weiner 1996).

Case study after case study emphasises the need for a strong institutional base for initiatives to flourish. Success ingredients at the school level include the support of the headteacher and other senior members of staff, as well as the political "muscle" provided by a dedicated working group. Indeed, it has been argued that those working in this area must be far more aware of the politics of the management of change, in terms of building support and alliances (Gaine 1989). In the late 1990s schools will have histories of past attempts at introducing equal opportunities policies, which can be positive or negative factors in the change process (Ruddock 1994). In a climate of increasing accountability, it is also important to build policies into the normal process of curriculum review, evaluation and institutional self-appraisal and inspection (Riley 1994).

Although many teachers express scepticism about the value of educational research, the increasing emphasis on institutional self-review has given a greater number of teachers the confidence to carry out research themselves (Millman 1987). Award-bearing and short in-service courses have also helped to equip teachers with more rigorous research and evaluation techniques, which can greatly enhance work in this area. Projects which have involved classroom observation, exploring children's attitudes through creative writing, personal constructs or formal questionnaires, or monitoring patterns of subject uptake have tended to be the most successful bottom-up approaches (see Whyte 1985; Gibbs 1989; Tutchell 1990). However, there is also increasing pressure to produce quantifiable and tangible results over a short period. This can be achieved when monitoring recruitment to subject areas, school-leaver destinations, or results attained in single-sex teaching groups (see, for example, James and Young 1989; Ruddock 1994). Yet much of the desired change in this area is long term, incremental, and hard to quantify, and as in the Netherlands, lack of evaluation remains problematic.

Despite exhortations to involve parents and governors in several published accounts, it is remarkable that so few actually include any detailed documentation of this, especially in a decade in which parents are being increasingly recruited as a force in educational change. One experiential account by a parent, who was herself a teacher, reported mixed parental reactions to her attempts to raise equal opportunities issues at the primary school gate (Rose 1989). Many parents expressed the view that they "just wanted their child to be happy" or felt that it was their own responsibility to provide models of appropriate behaviour at home. It was also those parents who had "authority" in the eyes of the school, through PTA involvement or having an academically successful child, who tended to take up such issues. It would not be surprising if this created a degree of resentment among others with fewer cultural resources. Another project, which tried to incorporate parents in the change process on collaborative terms, was described by the teachers involved as being "not an easy option .... we often feel as if we are walking uphill in deep snow, while being bombarded with snowballs" (Watson 1993, p. 185). Most parental concern appears to focus on girls' access to computers. Some parents are also worried about attempts to make their sons more "feminine" (Arnot, David, and Weiner 1996).

Initiatives at the upper levels of secondary education and in higher education have tended to be dominated by the issue of access to science and technology. Although boys are under-represented in certain subject areas, such as modern languages, this issue receives little public attention and concern. With the introduction of a more comprehensive national curriculum in England and Wales than in the divided structure of Dutch secondary education, there were hopes that this would stave off subject specialisation to a later stage. However, it is likely that a common curriculum will prove to be a necessary rather than sufficient condition for changes in subject uptake and that the weight of wider cultural and social factors will prove to be substantial. As in the Netherlands, the conclusion of many of the national projects at this level is that they have been more successful in changing attitudes than in having a direct effect on study choices. Nevertheless, there have been some demonstrable changes in such patterns in recent years. At the age of 16 and older there has been an increased female entry rate in the "male" sciences of physics, computer sciences and mathematics, and an increased male entry rate into the arts and modern languages. At the ages of 17 to 18 and older there has been a decreasing gender gap in favour of males in biology and females in the humanities and art and design, but an increased male entry rate in physics, technology, economics and computer studies, as well as in English and modern languages. Girls have greatly improved their performance in all subject areas and the gap between male and female performance levels at public examinations is closing (Arnot, David, and Weiner 1996). This has given rise to a renewed concern for the "disadvantaged" boy, fanned by media attention, a phenomenon also experienced in the Netherlands.

In further and higher education, there has been a high level of declared institutional commitment to equal opportunities, but wide variation in practice. Over 90 percent of further and higher education institutions have equal opportunities policies. Only a small proportion have the institutional mechanisms necessary to monitor or implement these policies fully (HMI 1991).

In further education, the main growth areas have been the screening of recruitment literature for gender imagery and in the expansion of special "access" courses for students with nonstandard qualifications for entry into higher education. Networks of women lecturers are increasingly providing lateral support for women working in the sector, but often in an "inhospitable psychological climate" (Warwick and Williamson 1989, p.34). The uncoupling of colleges of further education from LEA (Local Education Authority) control in 1993 may well result in less vigorous support for equal opportunities policies.

In the higher education sector, 93 percent of U.K. universities had equal opportunities policies in 1994, while 75 percent had monitoring systems in place (Wright 1994). The development of such policies was given a particularly high profile by pressure from the Committee of Vice Chancellors and Principals in 1991 and it has become almost de rigueur to have one. In practice, they cover a wide range of definitions and understandings of equal opportunities and specific strategies. They are often limited to low-cost measures, such as the introduction of codes of practice, and usually rely on voluntary co-operation. Examples of initiatives include the provision of child-care facilities, policies and procedures concerning harassment, language guidelines, staff and student recruitment, and curriculum initiatives such as women's studies courses. Most progress has been made in the "new" universities, which were formerly under LEA control. Although substantial improvements have been reported in some institutions in the 1990s there is also some evidence of apathy and hostility, especially towards what is perceived as positive discrimination, or a relegation of equal opportunities in terms of funding and policy priorities (Farish et al. 1995).

Policy and Practice Compared: a Summary

The development of an equal opportunities policy in the Netherlands has been greatly enhanced by the comparatively high level of commitment demonstrated by the Dutch government. Pro-active in generating social and educational policy in this area, it has given the issue of equal opportunities an official legitimacy and status which is lacking in England and Wales. However, the looser framework of the Dutch curriculum and the institutional autonomy guaranteed by the structure of the Dutch education system, has meant that the extent of potential jurisdiction over educational practice is weaker in the Netherlands than in England and Wales, at a time when the balance of power is shifting from the LEAs to the centre. As a consequence, the desired cascade effect of policy implementation has had mixed results, with evidence of variable support at the local level. The balance between specific and "facet" policy-making at the national level in the Netherlands is reflected in debates at the LEA and institutional level in England and Wales, concerning the tension between the permeation of equal opportunities into mainstream practice and the need to maintain a high and distinctive profile.

In England and Wales the lack of a central driving force at the ministerial or central state level or systematic infrastructure for the delivery of equal opportunities has been to some extent counterbalanced by thoughtful policy implementation at the local state level, where efforts have been made to combine top-down with bottom-up approaches. With the diminished power of the LEAs this influence is likely to change. In both countries, enthusiastic pressure groups have met with a mixture of teacher receptiveness, apathy, or even hostility, which suggests that a more considered approach to the management of change at this level is essential. In both countries there has been little research into parental attitudes and insufficient attention paid to the development of strategies for gaining public support. More careful monitoring and evaluation of implementation programmes and dissemination of results could be of benefit here, especially in an increasingly cost-conscious climate. However, many of the desired changes in this area are not limited to short-range, tangible results and are not directly amenable to quantitative evaluation. There thus remains a tension between being seen to "deliver the goods" and the pursuit of more fundamental change.

In terms of the presentation of equal opportunities issues, the 1979, 1985, and 1993 Dutch Ministry of Education policy documents have reflected an interpretation of the equal opportunities agenda which was not limited to the issue of subject choice. The aims of re-evaluating traditionally feminine qualities and enhancing the "care-independency" of boys have been absent from official discourse in England and Wales. Even if these aims have not resulted in a substantial change of practice, they nevertheless represent a wider understanding of gender inequalities than one in which girls are blamed for making the "wrong" subject and career choices. However, in both countries, the area where equal opportunities initiatives have made the most headway is in the extension of opportunities in science and technology to both sexes. The inclusion of these areas in the national curriculum from the age of five years in England and Wales will probably have a more significant impact than the more cautious changes recommended by the Dutch government. Although the maximisation of opportunities for girls and young women in scientific and technological pursuits is an important issue, this does not address the range of problems which women are likely to face in the labour markets of both countries in the late 1990s and beyond, where the creation of a more flexible workforce may accentuate the existing divisions in paid employment between men and women. The limited scope of such policy also does little to address the issues which surround the sphere of unpaid labour, where traditional attitudes are forged. That a more radical understanding of equal opportunities appears to impede the absorption of initiatives into mainstream educational practice in both countries poses a profound dilemma for those committed to change in this area.

References

Agnew, D., M. Booth, D. Kane, D., and E. Leitch. 1989. Case study: Equal opportunities and the Sheffield Curriculum Development Initiative (LAPP). In H. Burchell and V. Millman, eds., *Changing Perspectives on Gender: New Initiatives in Secondary Education.* Milton Keynes, Open University Press.

Arends, J., and H. Volman. 1992. A comparison of different policies: Equal opportunities in education in the Netherlands and the policy of the Inner London Education Authority *Gender and Education* 4(1–2): 57–66.

Arnot, M. 1987. Political lip-service or radical reform? In M. Arnot and G. Weiner, eds., *Gender and the Politics of Schooling.* Milton Keynes: Open University Press.

Arnot, M., M. David, and G. Weiner. 1996. *Educational Reforms and Gender Equality in Schools.* Manchester: Equal Opportunities Commission.

Askew, S., and C. Ross. 1988. *Boys Don't Cry: Boys and Sexism in Education.* Milton Keynes: Open University Press.

Browne, N., and P. France. 1986. *Untying the Apron Strings*. Milton Keynes: Open University Press.

Carr, C. 1989. The EOC's formal investigation into Initial Teacher Training. Report by the Equal Opportunities Commission Conference, *Equal Opportunities and Initial Teacher Training*. Manchester: EOC.

Claire, H., J. Maybin, J., and J. Swann. 1993. *Equality Matters: Case Studies from the Primary School*. Clevedon: Multilingual Matters.

Cunnison, S., and C. Gurevitch. 1990. Implementing a whole school equal opportunities policy: A primary school in Humberside. *Gender and Education* 2(3): 283–96.

Dekkers, H. 1990. Seksespecifieke Studiekeuzen in het Wetenschappelijk Onderwijs [Gender-specific subject choice in Higher Education]. Nijmegen: Instituut voor Toegepaste Sociale Wetenschappen.

Dekkers, H. 1994. Equal opportunities in education and the economic independence of women in North-West Europe. In G. Driessen, and P. Jungblath, eds., *Educational Opportunities: Tackling Inequality through Research*. Munster: Waxmann.

Dekkers, H. 1996. Determinants of gender-related subject choice. A longitudinal study in secondary education. *Educational Research and Evaluation* 2(2): 105–209.

Dekkers, H.. F. van Lieshout, and M. Stortelder. 1989. Onderwijskansen voor Meisjes uit Minderheden [Equal Opportunities for Minority Girls]. Nijmegen: Instituut voor Toegepaste Sociale Wetenschappen.

Department for Education and Employment (DfEE). 1996. *Education Statistics for U.K., 1995*. London: HMSO.

European Commission Network on Childcare. 1996. *A Review of Services for Young Children in the European Union 1990–1995*. Brussels: European Commission.

Farish, M., J. McPake, J. Powney, and G. Weiner. 1995. *Equal Opportunities in Colleges and Universities*. Ballmoor: Open University Press/ SRHE.

Gaine, C. 1989. On getting equal opportunities policies and keeping them. In M. Cole, ed., *Education for Equality. Some Guidelines for Good Practice*. London: Routledge.

Gibbs, J. 1989. Equal opportunities in Leicestershire. In C. Skelton, ed., *Whatever Happens to Little Girls?*. Milton Keynes: Open University Press.

Headlam-Wells, J. 1985. "Humberside goes neuter": An example of LEA intervention for equal opportunities. In J. White et al., eds, *Girl Friendly Schooling*. London: Methuen.

Hernwood, E. 1996. Wise choices? Understanding occupational decision making in a climate of equal opportunities for women and science. *Gender and Education* 8(2): 199–214.

Her Majesty's Inspectorate (HMI), 1991. *Equal Opportunities in Education: A Survey of Good Practice in England and Wales*. London: HMSO.

Jackson, D., and J. Salisbury. 1996. Why should secondary schools take working with boys seriously? *Gender and Education* 8(1): 105–16.

James, C., and J. Young. 1989. Case study: Equal opportunities through the Hertfordshire TVEI project. In H. Burchell and V. Millman, eds., *Changing Perspectives on Gender: New Initiatives in Secondary Education*. Milton Keynes, Open University Press.

Kelly, A. 1987. Traditionalists and trendies: Teachers' attitudes to educational issues. In G. Weiner and M. Arnot, eds., *Gender under Scrutiny: New Inquiries in Education*. London: Hutchinson.

Kirp, D., M. Yudof, and M. S. Franks. 1987. Gender in the house of policy. In M. Arnot and G. Weiner, eds., *Gender and the Politics of Schooling*. Milton Keynes: Open University Press.

Measor, L., and P. Sikes. 1992. *Gender and Schools*. London: Cassell.

Millman, V. 1987. Teacher as researcher: A new tradition for research on gender. In G. Weiner & M. Arnot., eds, op. cit.

Ministerie van Sociale Zaken en Werkgelegenheid. 1992. Beleidsprogramme Emancipatie "Met het oog op 1995" [Policy programme for emancipation with a view to 1995]. Den Haag.

Ministry of Social Affairs and Employment. 1995. *Women in the Netherlands: Facts and Figures*. The Hague.

Ord, F., and J. Quigley. 1985. Anti-sexism as good educational practice: What can feminists achieve? In G. Weiner, ed., *Just a Bunch of Girls*. Milton Keynes: Open University Press.

Plantenga, J. 1995. Labour Market Participation of Women in the European Union. In A. van Doorne-Huiskes, J. van Hoof, and E. Roelofs, eds., *Women and the European Labour Markets*. London: Paul Chapman Publishing.

Pot, L. 1995. Policies for children and parents in four European countries. In A. van Doorne-Huiskes et. al., op.cit.

Pratt, J., J. Bloomfield, and C. Searle. 1984. *Option choice: a Question of Equal Opportunity*. Slough: NFER/Nelson.

Reay, D. 1990. Working with boys. *Gender and Education* 2(3): 269–82.

Reay, D. 1993. "He doesn't like you, Miss." Working with boys in an infant classroom. In H.J. Claire, J. Maybin, and J. Swann. 1993. *Equality Matters: Case Studies from the Primary School*. Clevedon: Multilingual Matters.

Redman, P. 1994. *Shifting Ground: Rethinking Sexuality Education*. Buckingham: Open University.

Riley, K. 1994. *Quality and Equality. Promoting Equal Opportunities in Schools*. London: Cassell.

Rose, J. 1989. A parent's voice. In C. Skelton, ed., *Whatever happens to Little Girls?* Milton Keynes: Open University Press.

70   Gender Issues in International Education:Beyond Policy

Ruddock, J. 1994. *Developing a Gender Policy in Secondary Schools.* Buckingham: Open University.

Sikes, P. 1991. Nature took its course. Student teachers and gender awareness. *Gender and Education* 3(2): 145–62.

Skelton, C. 1989. Gender and initial teacher education, in C. Skelton, ed., *Whatever happens to Little Girls?* Milton Keynes: Open University Press.

Social Trends. 1995. London: HMSO.

Thompson, B. 1989. Teacher attitudes: Complacency and conflict. In C. Skelton, ed., *Whatever happens to Little Girls?* Milton Keynes: Open University Press.

Trickett, D. 1989. Leeds Primary Needs Programme and gender. In C. Skelton, ed., *Whatever happens to Little Girls?* Milton Keynes: Open University Press.

Tutchell, E., ed. 1990. *Dolls and Dungarees,* Milton Keynes: Open University Press.

Volman, M, E. van Eck, and G. ten Dam. 1995. Girls into science and technology: The development of a discourse. *Gender and Education* 7(3): 283–92.

Warwick, J., and A. Williamson. 1989. *Equal Opportunities (Gender) Policy and Practices in Colleges of Further Education.* London: Further Education Unit Research Report no. 505.

Watson, P. 1993. Parents and equal opportunities. In H.J. Claire, J. Maybin, and J. Swann. 1993. *Equality Matters: Case Studies from the Primary School.* Clevedon: Multilingual Matters.

Weiner, G. 1989. Feminism, equal opportunities and vocationalism: The changing context. In H. Burchell and V. Millman, eds., *Changing Perspectives on Gender: New Initiatives in Secondary Education.* Milton Keynes: Open University Press.

Weiner, G. 1990. *The Primary School and Equal Opportunities: International Perspectives on Gender Issues.* London: Cassell.

Whyte, J. 1985. Girl-friendly science and the girl-friendly school. In J. Whyte et al., eds., op. cit.

Wilson, M. 1990. *Girls and Young Women in Education: A European Perspective.* Oxford: Pergamon Press.

Wright, A. June 24, 1994. A sisterly hand up the ladder, Times Higher Educational Supplement, no. 1129, 13. In *Colleges of Further Education,* London: Further Education Unit Research Report no, 505.

CHAPTER 4

Australian Boys at Risk? The New Vocational Agendas in Schooling[1]

Jane Kenway, Peter Watkins and Karen Tregenza

Introduction

This chapter examines the well-popularised and increasingly popular claims that boys are at risk in the mid-1990s. It argues that while there are grains of truth in such claims, they are also simplistic and unhelpful for educational policy makers and teachers. The case is made for a more nuanced understanding of gender and risk in the context of widespread social change. This argument is advanced with particular reference to vocational education policies for schools. We begin the chapter with a discussion of changing times and their implications for policy with particular reference to vocational education and gender reform policies. Next we explore the concept of risk as it has been applied to boys, to "students at risk" and to "risk society". We then focus on the issue of vocational education, gender and risk and introduce the empirical work from which this chapter is drawn. Under this heading we consider the gendered dimensions of three areas of social change and their implications for vocational education: risk, autonomy, security and trust; the restructuring of certain transitions; and gender convergence and intensification.

Uncertainty, redefinition and restructuring

The British sociologist Anthony Giddens (1991) calls this era "the age of uncertainty". Hugh MacKay (1993), the Australian social commentator, calls it the "age of redefinition". Ulrich Beck, a sociologist from Germany talks of "risk society " (1992). Policy makers the world over are constantly engaged in restructuring. Those in educational circles are regularly restructured, redefined and uncertain. Risk and insecurity are features of their lives. Yet the search for certainty and the need to trust remain and remain elusive. Changing gender identities and relations, changing labour processes and labour markets and changing family forms are among the interrelated characteristics of this age.

In Australia as in other advanced Western economies, a feature of changing labour processes and labour markets is the decline of heavy (male-dominated) manufacturing, the rise of the retail and service sector (dominated numerically by females), and the decline in the influence of unions and thus of working conditions. A related feature is what Bakker (1996, p. 7) calls the "gender paradox of restructuring" — the "contradictory effects of the dual process of gender erosion and intensification." On the one hand we see the gendered polarisation of labour markets. Certain core, traditionally male, labour markets are shrinking, and certain peripheral, traditionally female, labour markets are expanding, hence gender differences in work are intensified. On the other hand we see the gendered convergence of labour market experiences. More workers, both male and female, are in poorly paid, part-time, nonunionised casual work. Beck (1992, p. 143) calls this the "generalisation of employment insecurity." Jobs traditionally filled by men are being downgraded and filled by women, but also, for want of something better, we see males moving into traditionally female jobs.

Despite the collapsing distinction between breadwinners and homeworkers and "the end of work" (Rifkin 1995) for some, women continue to carry the major load of household and emotional labour. This is so, even though there is some evidence of change in households characterised by intermittent patterns of employment and unemployment by males. Further, the decline of heavy industry has been of significance to certain single-industry localities. Such regions are being emptied of major sources of employment. Locality has thus become a particularly important factor in youth employment and unemployment.

Vocational education and gender reform have, both wittingly and unwittingly, been caught up in these changes. Let us consider how.

Policies for Vocational Education

New approaches to vocational education have quite dramatically altered the transition from schools to work in a context of extensive training, workplace and labour market restructuring (Kenway and Willis 1995).

Within Commonwealth and state educational policy in Australia, schools are now expected to change the mix of general and vocational education in order to strengthen the vocational, they are to provide greater clarity about the pathways between school education and a range of post-school destinations, and they are to help ensure that these pathways actually lead somewhere by enabling students to gain credentials which are acceptable in workplaces and in further education or training. Teenagers are encouraged to complete a full secondary education and to ensure that the education they receive in the post-compulsory years provides them with the "education and training capital" they need to enter the labour market or further education.

To be more specific, under the Commonwealth Labour Government (1983–1996), a series of reports associated with the National Training Reform Agenda (NTRA) argue for the development of more flexible pathways between education, training and employment. These seek to promote the integration and/or articulation of school and Technical and Further Education (TAFE) and/or private provider programmes with each other and with work-based and work-placement programmes (see Employment and Skills Formation Council 1992; Australian Education Council 1991). They propose an alignment of post-compulsory schooling, structured training and demonstrated work skills and the development of a Standards Framework. The purpose is to:

1. enable educators from different education and training sectors to focus on desirable vocational outcomes and develop curriculum to suit such outcomes;
2. allow a consistent approach to the assessment and reporting of young people's achievement in the key competencies;
3. assist in creating clearer linkages between education, training, and industry; and
4. provide new ways for industry to clarify its expectations of young people and the education and training system (see further, Kenway and Willis, 1995).

In addition, D.S. Karpin's report (1995) "Enterprising Nation: Renewing Australia's Managers to Meet the Challenges of the Asia Pacific Century," places a strong emphasis on enterprise education in schools, the vocationalisation of the general curriculum and the celebration of enterprise culture. In line with such thinking a new certificate of education course of study called "Industry and Enterprise Studies" has been developed in the Australian state of Victoria. It aims to teach students about work and its place in Australian industry and society. The study looks at the economic and social aspects of work. Students complement their theoretical understanding with experience gained through work placement, which allows them to develop skills and knowledge in a workplace setting. However, the overall emphasis of Industry and Enterprise Studies is the production of enterprising individuals.

Undoubtedly a significant influencing factor in the changes to vocational education programmes since 1993 has been the development of employment-related "Key Competencies" and "Competency Based Training" (CBT). The Mayer Committee's publication, *Putting General Education to Work – the Key Competencies Report*, proposed a set of seven Key Competencies that young people need to be able to participate effectively in the emerging forms of work and work organisation. It also established principles to provide for nationally consistent assessment and reporting of achievement of the Key Competencies (Mayer 1992). In contrast, CBT is directed towards the development of specific competencies for specific industries (see Employment and Skills Formation Council 1992).

The Labour approach has been revised under the recent (1996) Liberal/National Party government, which has developed the New Apprenticeship Scheme (NAS). While it is not at all clear how this will relate to the Labour initiatives, it appears that the school will be a central link in NAS. Young people will be able to undertake apprenticeships, traineeships or specific vocational courses as part of their school programme. It is expected that students will leave school having been trained in some work-related skills or even having completed part of a vocational education qualification. Consequently the Budget Paper of 1996 stresses that:

> Vocational education and training will be expanded in schools. Programmes will be developed that provide progress towards and lead into apprenticeships and traineeships. Students will be able to begin apprenticeships and traineeships while at school, to give senior secondary students a clear and accessible pathway to employment and further learning. [Moreover], the expansion of vocational education in schools and the further development of pathways from school to work will be supported through the provision of additional financial assistance to school systems to increase the number of appropriately trained teachers (Kemp 1996b, pp. 9–10).

It is expected that NAS will address the fact that the number of young people in apprenticeships is the lowest for three decades with just over 50,000 in apprenticeships and 20,000 in traineeships in 1995.

As result of all the above, we now see an increasing articulation of post-compulsory schooling, structured training and competency-based work-placement programmes. This has resulted in complicated, multisite, multisubject, multiassessment, dual accreditation and dual recognition programmes, school industry links through traineeships and apprenticeships, and enterprise curricula and programmes.

Policies for gender reform

Recent approaches to vocational education policy seek, in part, to address the needs of "students at risk". Most often these students are defined as disadvantaged, but their gender is ignored. In contrast, shifts in *general* gender reform policies for schools have sought to contribute to and address both the redefinition of gender identities and relations and, implicitly in recent times, the uncertainties which have arisen for boys as a result (see, for example, Gender Equity Taskforce, MCEETYA, 1996). However, implicit in such policies is the notion that the redefinition of gender noted earlier has placed boys *as a group* "at risk".

In contrast yet again, the more focussed gender reform polices for vocational education have conventionally perceived this as the domain of (working-class) boys and as most problematic for girls. The gender issues most commonly considered include the gendered segmentation of the vocational education curriculum in line with the gender segmentations of the labour force; the low representation in vocational courses of girls in comparison with boys; the incompatibility of many jobs with future family responsibilities and the implications of this for young women's career "choices"; the limited understandings of gender issues among career advisers and issues associated with sexual harassment in work experience sites (see further, Kenway and Willis 1995). Recently the gendered construction of skill and of workplace cultures has been acknowledged in policy.

The main and rather flawed policy response to such issues over the years has been informed by feminist versions of human capital theory and has encouraged girls to take up "non-traditional" subject and career pathways in the search for economic security, independence and mobility (see further, Kenway, 1993). However, frequent reports of hostile male environments and harassment have clarified the risks involved for "non-traditional" girls in traditional male environments. In such policies, the possible incompatibility of many jobs with future family responsibilities is too often not acknowledged, or seen as something to be escaped, rather than resolved. Equally, such thinking fails to address the definitions of valued or useful knowledge and what counts as "being skilled". Only recently have Australian policies for gender reform sought to develop a more nuanced vocational agenda, but as we have found in our research schools (discussed later), these have had little impact. However, given the hollowing out of the welfare state and with it the drying up of state support for gender reform, they appear unlikely to have much impact in the future.

Risk

The concept "at risk" is frequently employed in education circles at school and system levels. It has become a catch-all term for teachers and bureaucrats, one that is seldom adequately unpacked with regard to matters of gender, class, or other differences and dominances. As a result, the specificities and differences among those considered to be "at risk" are often overlooked. Further, the implications for education of "risk society" are similarly overlooked. This has unfortunate implications for both policy and practice. What do we learn if we consider "risk" more fully by drawing on the work of those who have sought to put some flesh on its bones?

The popular case about "boys at risk" has two main dimensions. Boys are portrayed as failing at school and failing at life. In comparison with girls, boys are seen to underachieve and to have more motivational and behavioural problems — they commit more crimes, have more road accidents, and commit suicide at a greater rate than girls. Further, they are said to lack social and emotional skills. The failing-at-life arguments have generated a body of interpretive research which explores the risks as well as rewards for boys of subscribing to particular versions of masculinity (see for example, Mclean 1997). It shows how risk and reward are often alternative sides of the same coin. For example, taking risks as a male may mean not taking risks with one's masculinity. The arguments about boys' comparative underachievement have been convincingly undermined by the wide-ranging statistical studies of Teese, Davies, Charlton and Polesel (1995). Their research challenges the popular assumption that girls overall are gaining more success through school than boys. It concludes that boys rely less on school because they have stronger vocational educational pathways outside it, that girls' patterns of subject success and choice offer them less tertiary study and career "pay off" than those of boys because they are less coherent, vocational and less mutually supporting.

All that said, it is important to observe that the discussion of boys at risk usually centres on the "academic" curriculum and does not attend to the "vocational". The implications of girls' and boys' relative success at school for their paid work options are not usually part of popular discussion. However, as we have shown elsewhere (Kenway and Willis 1995), if one is to compare the school and post-school *vocational* pathways taken by boys and girls, then girls have historically been at a disadvantage relative to boys and this state of affairs continues. Further and most importantly in terms of notions of risk, Teese et al. (1995) observe that gender differences sharply increase the more the social disadvantage of parents. They thus conclude that, "the real question is not whether girls as a group or boys as a group are more disadvantaged but which girls and which boys" (p. 109).

This point becomes more poignant and telling with regard to matters of "students at risk" when we consider issues associated with youth employment, unemployment, and underemployment. Both Freeland (1996) and Sweet (1995) outline statistically, the uncertainties, vulnerabilities and risks that young people are exposed to in their various pathways to the workplace. They draw particular attention to the risks which await those who do not try to enter full-time post-compulsory education but seek to enter the labour market instead. Sweet points to the different ways in which young people are marginalised from the mainstream of employment, education and training. *Unemployment*, that is wanting a job and not being able to find one, is the most common cause. Young people are also marginalised through solely relying on *casual part-time work*. They normally rely on jobs that provide only a few hours of poorly paid part-time work each week. The numbers in this category have "trebled from around five percent to over fifteen percent of all those young people who are not full-time students in the last five years" (1995, p. 6). Further, Sweet indicates that one in five has completely *dropped out* of both the labour market and education. They are not working, not looking for work, and not studying. Some can be traced through social security but others are simply "*lost*". It is suggested that this is partly a result of the increasing retention rates in schools, resulting in a labour market that relies more heavily on credentials. Accordingly, lower academic achievers and other disadvantaged groups are likely to have particular difficulty in competing for work (Sweet 1995, p. 7).

Recently, David Kemp, the Commonwealth Minister for Schools, Vocational Education and Training, observed that among 19 year olds, those who had not completed their schooling and had no vocational qualification had an unemployment rate close to 27 percent, those who had completed secondary school had an unemployment rate close to 18 percent, and those who held a vocational qualification had an unemployment rate of 7 percent (Kemp, 1996a). The Minister then argued:

> The senior secondary curriculum clearly needs to respond to the needs of the students for whom an academic course is not attractive. To provide opportunities for these students it is essential that schools offer pathways to training and employment and just as important that students think of schooling as providing that pathway (Kemp 1996b, p. 2).

Many teachers and policy makers think similarly and thus define "students at risk" as those who appear unlikely to complete secondary schooling. It is our opinion that this is a rather limited view.

Freeland (1996) argues that risk is constructed through the transition from childhood to adulthood, which "involves the provisional resolution of a range of questions relating to personal morality, sexuality, politics and economics, all of which contribute to one's personal identity" (1996, p. 7). He makes the case that the long-term structural collapse of the teenage labour market has:

> ... severely dislocated these processes. The experience of transition has been prolonged for all young people, and there is an identifiable stage of life wedged between adolescence and adulthood but the experience of this transition is not uniform. It is marked by complexity of inter-related social divisions based on class, gender, race, ethnicity and region, and this combination of factors has placed at risk a significant proportion of teenagers at risk of not effecting a secure transition to adulthood (1996, p. 7).

In Australia, the group of students including both boys and girls who increasingly find it difficult to enter the labour market and who could be classified as most *at risk* of being unemployed, underemployed or even lost includes working-class students, students with disabilities and indigenous students (Sweet 1995).

Let us consider some wider understandings of risk. Beck (1992) is concerned with a new self-endangering civilisation, which he terms "risk society." Beck defines risk as follows. First, he refers to the physical hazards, such as pollutants, radioactivity, chemicals in the food chain, for example, which are threatening life on this planet. These risks are seen as not merely the side effects of progress in the modern world; they *are* progress. Second, current times have brought a seductive and confusing array of new choices of work, family and lifestyle as the socialising agencies of society alter and as traditional values and linkages are eroded. Sources of identity and esteem are in greater number and are less fixed than in earlier times. Biography becomes an individual project constructed through apparently infinite but constrained and elusive choices. However, freedom from old constraints generates new uncertainties. Who am I? Who is in charge? What is my place in this world? Increased choice and autonomy are accompanied by increased risk.

Risk society is concerned not so much with the distribution of material goods but with the distribution of choices and uncertainties or risks. In Beck's view, blind growth has resulted in inequalities which are increasingly evident in an "individualised" rather than social class form. Hence, in the risk society, life becomes a biographical project of maximising choice and minimising risk, individually. However, risks also have a generalisable quality:

> Some people are more affected than others by the distribution and growth of risks, that is, *social risk positions* spring up. In some of their dimensions these follow the inequalities of class and strata positions, but they bring a fundamentally different logic into play. Risks of modernisation sooner or later also strike those who produce or profit from them .... Socially recognised risks .... contain a peculiar political explosive: what *was* until now *considered unpolitical becomes political — the elimination of the causes in the industrialization process itself* (Beck 1992, pp. 23–4, italics in original).

Thus for many, these risks outweigh the benefits which might occur from unconstrained economic growth. The result, according to Beck, is increased market dependency and new forms of social control. Speaking of policy-making practices in the risk society, Beck argues that "risk management" becomes a major preoccupation which involves "discovering, administering, acknowledging, avoiding or concealing such hazards with respect to specifically defined horizons of relevance." He argues that as the risks increase so too do promises of security (1992, pp. 19–20).

Gender, risk and vocational education

This summary of perspectives on risk indicates that risk is a general cultural phenomenon with implications for all, but that there are cohorts of students consisting of both girls and boys who are particularly "at risk" in terms of their school life and their post-school work options and identities. Further, it shows that within this category, there are some who are more at risk in both respects than others. As indicated, class, gender, race, ethnicity, location and their relationship to education and employment are all implicated in the production of cohorts of young people "at risk". Thus to suggest that boys *as a group* are more at risk than girls *as a group* is to oversimplify the issue of risk in a most unhelpful manner. Nonetheless, if gender becomes a focus for analysis of the issue of young people at risk, there is much to consider, as indicated by our current research project titled, *The Construction of Gender within the New Vocational Agenda for Schools: Implications for Gender Construction, Relations and Reform.*[2]

Through a series of case and cameo studies of different schools and programmes, we are considering vocational education in changing economic, technological and institutional contexts with particular reference to masculinities, femininities and localities. Our research in three states of Australia in capital cities, provincial cities and rural and remote areas shows that there have been various responses to the policy imperatives noted above by differently located schools. In very difficult circumstances many dedicated teachers are struggling both to develop programmes and to resolve the many deep problems involved. Some are doing this better than others but either way, any critical comments to follow are offered in a spirit of support.

Some of the more elite schools have ignored the vocational imperative altogether. Some have simply added programmes for small numbers of students while others have adopted a whole-school approach to, say, enterprise education. In some schools vocational education is defined quite narrowly and in others it is seen to include the "hand, the head and the heart." In some cases schools have developed a wide range of partnerships and links with business and industry and with public and private providers of training programmes. In other instances the institutions have remained as separated as ever. Some schools have devoted many resources to the development of new programmes and have appointed senior staff to develop and promote the field. In some of these instances such schools are becoming or looking to become accredited providers of training programmes for populations other than school students. Some have also been very successful in attracting additional grants. In many such cases the vocational education programme is becoming a "marketing tool", used to "add value" to the school's image and to attract students in an increasingly competitive schooling environment in which numbers equal dollars and in which schools below a certain number of students may be targeted for closure. Given the problems noted above with regard to youth and employment, those schools which can develop programmes which deliver jobs feel that they will be very well placed to attract "clients". In contrast other schools struggle to deploy staff, mount programmes, and make cross-sectoral connections.

The schools which have adopted new vocational policy agendas with the greatest enthusiasm have tended to be those which serve students who are less securely placed on a route to university education. In some instances these are also schools which serve some of the most seriously disadvantaged neighbourhoods in Australia. Such schools, some metropolitan, some rural, some remote, are located in areas where unemployment is high and where local industry, to the extent that it exists, is unable and in some cases unwilling to provide employment to the locality's youth. In both these cases new approaches to vocational education are seen to provide powerful new opportunities to minimise the risks which plague these particular populations. These students have been encouraged to trust such programmes, to see them as "a step ahead, a foot in the door" (as described by a Year-12 boy involved in an industry-based/school apprenticeship programme).

As our research-in-progress is indicating, gender identities, relations and inequalities are integral to current processes and contexts of vocational education. Predictably, old gender issues remain and indeed in some cases have been exacerbated. However, as a function of all the changes noted above, new gender (and other) issues have emerged, many of which relate to risk and trust. These mean that those in the field must move beyond fashionable but facile and futile arguments about boys *as a group* at risk and ask questions that pertain to the differences within and across difference and to the complexities of these changing times. It is timely to ask "How are gender identities and inequalities inscribed within current approaches to vocational education? Are such inscriptions acceptable or should they change in the light of the times?" Many new issues relate to risk, trust and redefinition. Consider the following.

Experiences of risk, autonomy, security and trust

Are risk, autonomy, security and trust distributed differently between and within the sexes? For example, Sweet implies that through unemployment of various sorts, young people risk becoming economically dependent, living in poverty and risk succumbing to a host of associated problems. What do these different experiences of risk mean for the current construction of male and female identities and gender relationships among unemployed, underemployed and "lost" young people? What might these mean for vocational programmes through and beyond schools? How might vocational education help girls and boys to maximise gender choices and minimise gender risks, particularly in situations of dependency and poverty?

Vocational education today is a form both of risk management and minimisation, which implicitly makes very risky promises of security. As a vocational education co-ordinator in one of our schools says, the students who do the programme are the students willing to take a risk. The sense of risk reduction and lessening of anxiety involves what Giddens (1984, p. 50) terms "ontological security, expressing an autonomy of bodily control within predictable routines." Confidence is thereby created and the sense of risk reduced in such contexts. Trust, Giddens argues, (1984, p. 53) equals confidence with a definite sense of mutuality about it; "there is at least an incipient feeling of 'being trustworthy' associated with the generalised extension of trust to the other" (p. 53). Also, according to Giddens (1990, pp. 83–4) our uncertain, reflexive, future-oriented modern institutions and society are, of necessity, predicated on another level of trust: trust in abstract and expert systems.

If they are to work, new vocational education programmes with their complicated institutional and curriculum and assessment arrangements must instil such self/other trust in students who historically have every reason to distrust teachers and schools. Further, they must help them to understand some of the social implications for them of expert/abstract trust patterns. Thus trust must have many sides. Too often in our schools we see that it does not.

Students are encouraged to entrust their future to such programmes. Such trust becomes a programme's selling point to others. Students are not to put the programme and implicitly other students' futures at risk. Yet our data suggest that a lack and loss of trust is already evident among some of the boys and girls of our research schools:

- "There's lots of things they've promised that didn't come out. They almost dropped us in the deep end and left us there."
- "They dangle a big carrot in front of you. They offer you money to go to school. When we first started here they promised 8 apprenticeships and that's been dropped to 4. So they've halved that. They've also offered some assistance for those students who want to go to uni where that hasn't happened."
- "They say they want half girls and half boys in the programme but I don't think they really mean it."

Sometimes the programme is considered more important than students' experiences within it, as one girl found when she complained about harassment on work placement. She was not believed and urged not to place the programme at risk by taking the matter further. Trust/security and anxiety/risk are a feature of vocational education. In instances such as this, the latter are managed not minimised. Meanwhile, the gender lessons for the students are clear.

While Competency-Based Training (CBT) and Key Competencies may benefit such students by offering them "recognition of prior learning," pathways leading to credentials, and, possibly, a sense of being trustworthy, they do not necessarily provide them with the knowledge to better understand the world around them, let alone to challenge abstract/expert systems by, for example, developing a sense of industrial agency in the era of enterprise bargaining. The standing of competencies varied across the cameo schools in our study. Some felt competencies had outlived their usefulness and were to be surpassed by dual accreditation and/or dual recognition; while others developed their vocational education programmes around the seven Key Competencies, working closely with industry to both raise employer awareness, and to ensure a satisfactory assessment strategy for each party. Yet others used CBT in students' work placements and TAFE courses. We will have more to say on the matter of competencies later.

If we take a broader view of risk and understand it as a general cultural phenomenom, what are the implications for vocational education policy and practice? What are the implications for students who, in the first instance, may not regard themselves as at risk?

The restructuring of transitions

The restructuring of the transitions from school to work/post-school life and from adolescence to adulthood mean that the grounds upon which to build ontological security are uncertain. Giddens argues that the feelings of self doubt and worthlessness frequently exhibited by young people who are unemployed form a tension-management system around which the polarities of trust/security and anxiety/risk are organised.

Such trust-anxiety polarities are exemplified in his analysis of Willis' British study of working-class "lads" *Learning to Labour* (1977). Traditional curricula make the lads alienated and anxious and masculine; manual labour is considered preferable to the conformity and effeminacy associated with the "brain work" demanded by the school's traditional curricula. This leads them to resist it through the creation of an aggressive, joking anti-school culture which resembles the shop-floor culture of their future workplaces. It is this cultural identity, continuity, and stability which provides them with ontological security.

Hence, Giddens argues, "they find the adjustment to work relatively easy and they are able to tolerate the demands of doing dull, repetitive labour in circumstances they recognise to be uncongenial" (Giddens 1984, p. 293). Writing in the late 1970s, Willis points out that within the lads' culture there is a conception of the inevitability of work and of certain kinds of work "the apparent timelessness and inevitability of industrial organisation .... the hardness and inevitability of industrial work" (1977, p. 16).

How times have changed. More recently, Mac an Ghaill (1996), points out that young people in the 1990s, find themselves in a "new social condition of suspended animation between school and work. Many of the old transitions into work, into cultures and organisations of work, into being consumers, into independent accommodation — have been frozen or broken..." (1996, p. 390). Similarly, Freeland raises issues of identity and implies that without adequate work and income, young people cannot in effect grow up and become adults. Going further, Beck implies that the institutions that, in the traditional sense, defined growing up are losing their hold on the collective consciousness.

Most current vocational education programmes are multi-institutional and students are split across the different gendered mores of each institution.

> Although the trainers are good tradesmen, they're not good teachers. They were put in the deep end as much as we were. They need to train the people better. One trainer has been described as a sexist pig. He is not a very good person to have teaching guys because he passes his views on just in the way that he talks — that girls are inferior (Year 12 girl apprentice).

This process of splitting has particular implications for age and authority relations, for the traditional transitions from school to work and for the gendered identities that adolescents construct around them. As a Year-12 boy involved in an industry-based/school apprenticeship programme says:

> They're almost running the school like industry but we're still only kids.

Yet another such boys says:

It's hard. You try to make decisions for yourself and sometimes the teachers don't like that because they are used to teaching not negotiating. Whereas in the workplace you've got to make your own decisions. [In the workplace] you can often negotiate with the person who has given you the job whereas at school and in the training centre you can't.

How then, do differently located young women's experiences of these restructured transitions differ from those of differently located young men? Might they undermine many girls' increasing sense of freedom from gender traditions and reinscribe them as docile and dependent? And, given that masculinity has historically been so intimately connected with employment and with certain power positions within households, what do these transitions mean for boys? Given that it is no longer feasible for boys to hang onto traditional notions of wage and domestic labour, which involve male breadwinners and female home-workers, are new models of masculinity likely to arise in households and workplaces? Mac an Ghaill (1996) suggests that this is indeed happening in some cases in the U.K. but not for those boys who feel their masculinity most at risk. Further, how then do boys and girls construct their gendered biographies within this context of the restructuring of transitions? We have much to learn in this respect.

Gender erosion and gender intensification around work

What are the implications of gender erosion and intensification for masculinity and femininity and the relationships within and between them in the workplace and in vocational education? Consider two set of implications.

Such shifts have had particularly destructive implications for manual trades, long associated with apprenticeship, but which no longer guarantee employment. For those men whose manual labour is an important source of their masculinity these shifts have cut deeply into the foundations of their identity. This places in question those masculinities formed through manual work. Mac an Ghaill's (1996) research from the U.K. shows how certain traditional conceptions of working-class masculinity seem to be at risk and how others are emerging. It also sheds some light on the implications of this for vocational education. Blurring the distinction between vocational and general education is implicit in programmes for vocational policies. New hierarchies between high- and low-status vocational fields are developing in the U.K. and leading to the restratification of working-class male students. The emerging high-status technological and commercial subject areas such as business studies, technology, and computer studies are providing some such boys with what he calls an "ascending and modernising version of working-class masculinity" with associated values of "rationality instrumentalism, forward planning and careerism." Other working-class boys, he argues, are maintaining a descending traditional mode of masculinity based on low-level, practically-based subject areas which reflect the tough masculinity of jobs on the disappearing shop floor. The boys who subscribe to this mode of masculinity can be seen to be particularly "at risk". There is now an increasing amount of literature which suggests that as males lose power in one arena they search for new ways of expressing it in order to reclaim their sense of manhood. This suggests that boys at risk place themselves and others at greater risk. But what of girls?

Elsewhere (Kenway and Willis 1995), we have considered the implications for the post-school options of young women of Labour's policies for reshaping the post-compulsory curriculum to make it more oriented to the workplace. For example, we have made the case that the generic work-related Key Competencies proposed for the general curriculum have some potential to enhance girls' work options because:

1. they include competencies at which girls and women are generally considered to excel (eg., communicating ideas and information, working with others and in teams) but for which they often receive little credit;
2. they provide young women with the opportunity to document and accredit their competencies and thus to redress the imbalances in the rewarding of the skills that young women and young men have and which are involved in the work that young women and young men do;
3. they make explicit to all students what work-related competencies and the expectations of the workplace are. This may reduce the extent to which competence continues to be socially distributed according to gender, class and race;
4. they focus on what students actually can do rather than on where or how they learned to do it, thus the Key Competencies can benefit those young women who develop and exhibit their competencies in settings other than formal education or in areas of the curriculum which are less esteemed.

We argued that the Key Competencies have more potential to enhance girls' work options than the more narrow competencies proposed in CBT modules. However, we also expressed the view that vocational programmes specifically in and through schools may also be of benefit to girls because in many ways schools provide a more "girl-friendly" environment than industry or TAFE, and young women may be somewhat more likely to risk a non-traditional pathway in the relatively supportive environment of the school. This is particularly the case since school programmes are likely to maintain a sufficiently broad base in general education so that young women will be able to "try out" certain pathways without closing others off completely, an option which is not available within industry-based programmes. Further, schools are more likely to undertake programmes which have gender equity as an explicit objective and to work for social justice.

However, in the light of NAS the extent to which such potential will ever be actualised remains to be seen. Equally, it is not at all clear whether funding will be made available to address any of the other gender issues noted above. The NAS statement by the Commonwealth Minister for Schools, Vocational Education and Training in the August 1996 Budget purports to go some way towards addressing such problems as the severe disparity between males and females gaining access to the apprenticeship system. As Kemp explains:

> Through the introduction of part-time traineeships and new flexible arrangements, apprenticeship and traineeship opportunities for women will be expanded. Women will also benefit from the extension of apprenticeships and traineeships into areas where they have been generally unavailable but where there is a high concentration of women workers (often in part-time positions), such as in service industries (Kemp 1996a, p. 21).

On the surface of things this appears a reasonable move. Historically, young Australian women have been effectively excluded from most apprenticeships and have not usually had access to formal training as part of their jobs. Where training was available to women, as in business studies, it was either at the public or their own expense, prior to employment, and it generally led to lower status credentials than those available to young men. Even in the early nineties, almost 90 percent of the 16 percent of school leavers who went into apprenticeships were male, receiving a training wage and an undertaking of future employment. Of the 5 percent of school leavers who entered certificate courses, including Australian Traineeship holders, 70 percent were women. Trainees were paid three days a week and had only a reasonable prospect of future employment. Traineeships are counted in the statistics as full-time jobs; in fact, they currently make up one-third of full-time

female teenage employment. The majority of traineeships are in clerical
or retail work. Traineeships are one of the main avenues of employment
security for teenage women who do not go on to full-time tertiary study,
but they have been fewer in number and available in a narrower range
of employment areas than are apprenticeships and recipients earn less
than do apprentices. A little arithmetic on the figures shows that close to
16 percent of all male school leavers are paid to undertake training
through an apprenticeship or traineeship compared with 5 percent of all
female school leavers. While the NAS move may appear reasonable on
first glance, it only addresses the tip of the iceberg with regard to "girls
at risk" in an environment where boys are very clearly less so.

Conclusion

In the light of all we have said, we conclude first that the case that boys
per se are at risk can not be sustained but that the boys who are at risk
are those who come from the more disadvantaged end of the social scale
and who subscribe to traditional versions of masculinity. However, we
also conclude that the implications in the boys-at-risk thesis that girls are
no longer "at risk," particularly with regard to vocational education, can
not be sustained either. Indeed, this is one of the major implications of
this chapter, along with the assertion that gender education and reform
for girls and boys must be integral to vocational education. However, it
also our view that they must be rethought in order that they may better
meet the issues raised by the "end of certainty," "the age of redefinition,"
and the development of the "risk society."

Notes

1. This project is funded by the Australian Research Council and is being
   conducted by Jane Kenway, Peter Watkins, and Sue Willis, with Karen
   Tregenza as research associate.
2. We acknowledge the work of Peter Kelly in helping to establish the
   project.

References

Australian Education Council. 1991. *Listening to girls: A Report of the Consultancy Undertaken for the Review of the National Policy for the Education of Girls*. Carlton, Melbourne: Curriculum Corporation,

Australian Education Council. 1991. *Young People's Participation in Post-compulsory Education and Training*. Report of the Australian Education Council Review Committee (Brian Finn, Chairperson). Melbourne: AEC.

Bakker, I., ed. 1996. *Rethinking Restructuring: Gender and Change in Canada*. Toronto, Buffalo and London: University of Toronto Press.

Beck, U. 1992, *Risk Society: Towards a New Modernity*. London: Sage.

Commonwealth Schools Commission. 1975. *Girls, Schools and Society*. Canberra: AGPS.

Employment and Skills Formation Council. 1992. *Vocational Certificate Training*. The Carmichael Report. Canberra: National Board of Employment, Education and Training.

Freeland, J. 1996. Students (young people) at risk. Paper presented at the Making it Work: Vocational Education in Schools Conference, March 21 and 22, Melbourne.

Gender Equity Taskforce, MCEETYA (Ministerial Committee for Employment, Education, Training and Youth Affairs). 1998. *Gender Equity, A Framework for Australian Schools*. Australian Government Publishing Services: Melbourne, Australia.

Giddens, A. 1984. *The Constitution of Society*. Cambridge: Polity Press.

Giddens, A. 1991. *The Consequences of Modernity*. Cambridge: Polity Press.

Karpin, D.S. 1995. *Enterprising Nation: Renewing Australia's Managers to Meet the Challenges of the Asia Pacific Century*. Report of the Industry Taskforce on Leadership and Management Skills, Commonwealth of Australia.

Kemp, D. 1996a. *Training for Real Jobs: The Modern Australian Apprenticeship and Traineeship System*. Ministerial Statement, Budget. August, AGPS.

Kemp, D. 1996b. Educational opportunities for all. Address to the annual conference of the Australian Curriculum, Assessment and Certification Authorities. August, Canberra.

Kenway, J. 1993. Non-traditional pathways: Are they the way to the future? In J. Blackmore, and J. Kenway, eds., *Gender Matters in Educational Administration and Policy: A Feminist Introduction*. London and New York: Falmer Press, pp. 81–101.

Kenway, J., and S. Willis. 1995. *Critical Visions: Policy and Curriculum Rewriting the Future of Education, Gender and Work*. Canberra, Australia: Corporate Communications Section, Department of Employment Education and Training.

Kenway, J. with J. Blackmore, L. Rennie and S. Willis. 1997. *Answering Back: Girls, Boys and Feminism in Schools.* Sydney: Allen and Unwin and London: Routledge 1988.

Mac an Ghaill, M. 1996. "What about the boys?": Schooling, class and crisis masculinity. *Sociological Review* 44(3): 381–97.

MacKay, H. 1993. *Reinventing Australia: The Mind and Mood of Australia in the 90s.* Sydney, Australia: Angus and Robertson.

Mclean, C. 1997. Engaging with boys' experiences of masculinity: Implications for gender reform in schools. *Curriculum Perspectives.*

Meyer, E. 1992. *Putting General Education to Work: The Key Competencies Report.* Canberra: The Australian Education Council and Ministry for Vocational Education and Training, Australian Government Publishing Service.

Rifkin, J. 1995. *The End of Work: The Decline of the Global Labour Force and the Dawn of the PostMarket Era.* New York: G.P. Putnam's Sons.

Sweet, R. October 1995. All of their talents? Policies and programs for fragmented and interrupted transitions, *Dusseldorp Skills Forum.*

Teese, R., M. Davies, M. Charlton, and J. Polesel. 1995. *Who Wins at School?: Boys and Girls in Australian Secondary Education.* Melbourne: Department of Education Policy and Management, University of Melbourne.

Willis, P. 1977. *Learning to Labour.* London: Saxon House.

CHAPTER 5

Waiting for Government: The Implementation of Legislation on Gender Issues in the U.S.A.

Nelly P. Stromquist

Introduction

Feminists are divided about using the state to advance the situation of women. Some groups believe that the state must be pressured to pass laws to prevent sexual discrimination and to foster measures that will provide equity for women. Others are much less willing to rely on government action, believing that any intervention would either (a) be very weak and thus ineffectual, or (b) tend to reify rather than question the present social relations of gender. It has been the first group, usually termed the "feminist liberals," who have initiated political action. "Radical" and "social feminists," on the other hand, prefer to work at grassroots levels in the creation of new practices and the development of alternative gender identities, rather than relying on public laws and policies.

The major thrusts of the feminist movement in the United States in the last two decades have been to increase access of women to employment and to improve conditions for them in the labor force. The concern for maternity leave and child-care rights that accompanied the movement further pointed to women's role as workers. Formal education, despite its powerful capacity as both an ideologically reproductive and a socially transformative mechanism, received less attention than it deserved. Evidence of this can be seen in the objectives in the 1967 Bill of Rights of NOW, the National Organization for Women, the largest and most active feminist organization in the 1960s and 1970s. The attainment of "equal and unsegregated education" was the sixth objective in a list of eight.[1]

Through the mobilization of feminist groups, two major pieces of nationwide educational legislation were passed in the United States: Title-IX of the Educational Amendments Act of 1972 and the Women's Educational Equity Act (WEEA), enacted in 1975. These laws addressed problems of access to educational offerings and, to a lesser extent, issues of sociocultural transformation. They viewed girls and women as persons who had suffered unfair treatment. The contestation of dominant gender identities and the concomitant need to resocialize teachers and students on a massive scale was not contemplated. These two policies did not theorize an essentialist nature of women; on the other hand, they did not envisage an analysis of gender identity formation and how school mechanisms contribute to create fixed and asymmetric gender categories.

Title-IX offered the "stick" of the law, as it consisted of a set of rules and regulations that prohibited sexual discrimination in programs and activities of the educational system with the threat of cutting federal funds to institutions that did not comply. WEEA represented the "carrot" of the law in that it provided financial resources and technical assistance to encourage the design, adoption, and implementation of new programs that could create more gender-egalitarian environments in educational settings. This chapter examines the nature of these two pieces of legislation, their evolution over time, the implementation processes that have characterized them, and the kinds of achievements that can be attributed to them. It also analyzes the role of the state in framing the Title-IX legislation and affecting its outcomes.

Title-IX: Preventing Sexual Discrimination in Education

Title-IX affected educational institutions receiving federal funds, which is practically all institutions, although it exempted religious schools and religious universities. It was a comprehensive legislation whose prohibitions covered multiple institutional areas affecting students: admissions, recruitment, housing facilities, access to course offerings, counselling, financial assistance, employment, and athletics. It covered also employment issues concerning professional and clerical staff working for educational institutions. Title-IX was enacted after years of struggle by feminist groups. Ironically, this legislation was passed as an unnoticed addendum in a general bill. Its main clause reads:

> No person in the United States shall, on the basis of sex, be excluded
> from participation in, be denied the benefits of, or be subjected to

discrimination under any program or activity receiving Federal financial assistance.

The former Department of Health, Education, and Welfare (HEW) took three years to formulate the regulations accompanying this law (1972–1975) and four additional years to produce "policy interpretations" dealing with the issues of equity in athletics, an area that was hotly contested.

The regulations of Title-IX explicitly omitted consideration of texts and even curricular content. Thus, Section 86.42 of its regulations states:

Nothing in this regulation shall be interpreted as requiring, prohibiting, or abridging in any way the use of particular textbooks or curricular materials.

Avoidance of textbooks and curricula was justified in terms of a possible contradiction of the First Amendment of the Constitution, which guarantees freedom of speech. But it must be noted that there was also strong resistance by publishing houses, which through personal connections brought pressure to bear on the HEW's secretary of education to remove coverage of textbooks and curricula from the guidelines (The Editors, Harvard Educational Review 1979).

Enforcing the Law

Title-IX was assigned for enforcement to HEW's Office for Civil Rights (OCR). This agency had been in existence since the mid-1960s to enforce Title VI of the Civil Rights Act of 1964, which prohibits discrimination on the basis of race, color, and national origin. In addition to the Civil Rights Act and Title-IX, OCR was also assigned enforcement of Section 504 of the Rehabilitation Act of 1973, which prohibits discrimination on the basis of physical and mental handicap, and the Age Discrimination Act of 1975. Title-IX never received any special funds. Since OCR was a unit within HEW, its budget depended on internal allocations within the department and on the voluntary response by the various state educational agencies.

Title-IX guidelines, in addition to prohibiting sex discrimination, required that by 21 July 1976 (about one year after the appearance of the guidelines) every institution receiving federal assistance: appoint and publicize the name of its Title-IX co-ordinator, notify all students and employees that the institution did not discriminate on the basis of sex, start reviewing its programs and policies for non-sex discrimination, and begin developing grievance procedures for resolving sex discrimination problems.

Additional requirements included stating full compliance regarding physical education opportunities and competitive athletics, and presenting assurances of non-discrimination to OCR. Title-IX authorized affirmative or remedial action in instances in which a member of one sex needed to be treated differently to overcome the specific effects of past discrimination. Remedial action would be *ordered* by OCR or courts upon finding evidence of discrimination. Affirmative action would be *voluntary*, as the regulations noted that "a recipient [institution] may take affirmative action to overcome the effects of conditions which resulted in limited participation therein by persons of a particular sex."

OCR has ten regional offices responsible for complaint investigations, compliance reviews, monitoring of corrective action plans, and technical assistance to facilitate anti-discriminatory plans. OCR has operated with an annual budget of approximately $45 million, which in the view of its head was "insufficient to allow OCR to fund its full complement of FTE [full-time equivalent positions] during FY 1990 to maintain the full level of compliance activities" (OCR 1991 p. 3). Over the years, OCR has maintained a stable staff of 820 full-time members and processed about 3,500 complaints per year. Sex discrimination complaints have represented a small proportion of the complaints received by OCR (ranging from a low 3 percent in 1990 to a high 8 percent in 1994). Most complaints addressed to OCR have been those in the area of physical and mental disability. It is unclear at this point whether the small number of sex-based complaints reflects a lack of awareness of the law, a resolution of conflict at the local school or district level and thus the absence of need to bring it to the attention of OCR, or the belief that gender conditions are acceptable as they are.

Within education, most of the complaints have focused on discrimination in athletic programs (often intercollegiate sports). To a lesser extent there have been complaints of sexual harassment, and even fewer have been related to discriminatory pregnancy policies.

Judicial and Legislative Questioning of Title-IX

Over the years Title-IX was contested in federal courts to determine whether (a) individuals could sue institutions (Cannon v. University of Chicago); (b) whether employment was covered in the provisions (North

Haven v. Bell); (c) whether punitive damages were accessible to aggrieved parties (Lieberman v. University of Chicago); and (d) whether the law applied to programs only or to the entire educational institution (Grove City v. Bell). The courts decided that: (a) individual legal action was possible; (b) employment was covered; (c) punitive damages were not available; and (d) the entire institution was not affected by Title-IX. This last decision, ruled by the Supreme Court in 1984, was particularly damaging to Title-IX because it eliminated all possibility of conducting compliance reviews — a more pro-active way of seeking non-discriminatory sexual practices. It took a major effort by feminist groups, supported by progressive politicians — particularly Senator Edward Kennedy — to counter this Supreme Court decision. Through the passing of the Civil Rights Restoration Act in March 1988, it was stated that the "program and activity" wording of Title-IX referred to "all operations" of a department or agency of the state, university, local education agency, or corporation involved in education.[2] This legislation thus gave OCR jurisdiction to initiate an investigation of any institution receiving federal funds, but it came after four years of near paralysis in the implementation of Title-IX.

While the gains of Title-IX may have been modest, as we will discuss below, a significant bone of contention has been the application of Title-IX to athletics. The National Collegiate Athletic Association has been trying since its initial passage to exempt "revenue-producing sports" from Title-IX regulations. This effort has tended to put compliance reviews in secondary and higher education athletics on hold. Pressure has also been exerted by athletics departments from many schools and universities with substantial intramural or intercollegiate programs, which have argued that these male-dominated programs represent considerable revenues for their respective institutions or that girls have not been interested in sports in the same proportions as boys. On the other side, women have filed complaints and suits calling for equal distribution of funds for girls and boys in sports. In January 1996 a federal court rejected the "proportionality" principle, which had been established to put more women in certain sports.

By 1978 there was a 500 percent increase in the women's share of athletic budgets in secondary schools since 1972. At the post-secondary level, the proportion of women in athletics had risen from 2 percent in 1972 to 14 percent in 1978 (Sanborn 1983).

More recently, an increasingly widespread backlash has emerged. This has taken the form of anti-affirmative action efforts at the state level via propositions, that is, laws enacted by popular initiative rather than through the legislative process. One such successful measure took place in California through Proposition 209, passed in 1996. This proposition sought ostensibly to end "preferences" in hiring and contracting and in public education at the state level. In reality, it would enable employers to bypass the Civil Rights Act as well as Title-IX, since both authorize affirmative action in order to secure a more balanced labor force or student body. Clause (c) in Proposition 209 changed employment practices in the state from "a compelling state interest" to "reasonably necessary" to justify discrimination based on gender. A clear reading of this wording is that employers could now exclude women from non-traditional jobs such as working for the police force. The funding of programs providing equal access to girls' and boys' activities could suffer. The traditional gender stereotypes could be reaffirmed, since discrimination would work against both men and women when they seek jobs in fields dominated by the other sex.

A precursor to Proposition 209 was the decision on the Hopwood v. Texas case a few years earlier, in which the plaintiff challenged the admissions plan at the University of Texas Law School. This plan placed white and minority applicants on separate tracks to increase the number of minority students admitted. A federal court of appeals decided the approach was unacceptable and held that schools could no longer use race or ethnicity as factors in admissions. This decision represented a serious blow to a previous decision, Regents of the University of California v. Bakke (1978). In that ruling, the Supreme Court accepted special consideration of race through affirmative action to help candidates, but decided that fixed quotas by race were "unacceptably discriminatory."

Proposition 209 was upheld as constitutional by the Supreme Court in November 1997. In the meantime, Proposition 209 has succeeded in creating tension between two marginal groups: racial/ethnic minorities and women. Similar petitions to defeat affirmative action had been initiated and failed in Colorado, Delaware, Florida, Massachusetts, Oregon, and Washington. Also unsuccessful were 19 state legislative efforts during 1995–1996 to ban affirmative action. Both sides consider that successful implementation of Proposition 209 will encourage other stages to pass similar measures.

The American Civil Liberties Union has been fighting against the implementation of 209 on the grounds that it would undermine the U.S. Constitution since it would deny minorities and women preferential treatment (for example, the University of California continues to have preferences for students from certain counties in order to ensure geographical diversity, and for veterans to honor their service to their country) and prohibit public employers from complying with federal law that encourages voluntary measures to remedy and prevent race and sex discrimination (that is, Title-IX). The forthcoming decision by the Supreme Court will be of utmost importance.

Women's Educational Equity Act: Fostering More Gender-Sensitive Educational Environments

Feminist groups spent three years (1971–1974) of lobbying efforts before the WEEA law was enacted. It was passed as part of the Special Projects Act of 1974 and was extended in 1978, this time as part of the Educational Amendments of 1978. WEEA legislation has provided discretionary grants for projects to develop, evaluate, and disseminate curricula, textbooks, and other educational materials; to provide pre- and in-service teacher training; to improve guidance and promote quality of education for women at all levels of education; and to offer adult education for women, particularly those who are underemployed. Further amendments took place in 1984 so that WEEA could fund "comprehensive plans for implementation of equity programs at every educational level" (down to the local school districts) and "innovative approaches to school-community partnerships."

Initially the WEEA legislation was expected to provide sufficient financial resources so that school districts and states would be encouraged to create innovative educational environments to achieve gender equity. Its advocates expected that some $40 million would be available to carry out the program each year. However, at its inception WEEA was legislated as part of the Special Projects Act, and this Act was supposed to be funded for $200 million per year. When President Ford requested only $39 million for the Act, the share for WEEA became $6.3 million. Through the years, WEEA never came close to the funding requested by its proponents. It attained the highest level of funding at $10 million in FY 1981. It declined since then to $500,000 in 1992, a figure that was maintained until 1995 and which covered only the operating expenses of the WEEA Publishing Center, whose task it was to disseminate innovative materials. Major cuts in the 1996 federal budget resulted in zero funds for WEEA, although $2 million had been requested for FY 97.[3]

WEEA funds, which were made available for research and demonstration grants, were extremely competitive, with approximately 30 grants funded out of over 500 applications presented every year. The funds were allocated to either universities/research centers or state educational agencies; local school districts — the site with the most direct potential impact for changing primary and secondary school environments — received only minor amounts of WEEA funds. Most of the educational-equity activities conducted by the states and the local school districts have not been supported by WEEA, but rather through technical assistance from the Sex Desegregation Assistance Centers funded by Title IV of the Civil Rights Act of 1964 (Brown and Reid 1987), which provides both training and educational materials to reduce sex segregation, bias, and stereotyping. Initiatives at the state level have been weak because a substantial part of the costs must be borne by the states themselves. For instance, during FY 1992 the federal government covered 42 percent of the average state operating costs in all forms of equity measures (Brown and Reid 1987).

The funds available through WEEA enabled the development of gender-sensitive curriculum and teacher training materials. The most useful products were the training materials for administrators and teachers designed to familiarize educational staff with the rationale and methodology for implementing Title-IX. The design of materials for actual classroom use appears to have been less successful (Bornstein 1985). In all, WEEA has produced over 100 educational materials, ranging from texts to videotapes. These materials, however, have had limited circulation since only six of its publications have printed more than 3,000 copies, of which three printed more than 5,000 (Applied Systems Institute, 1985).

An important initiative supported by the WEEA legislation was the development of national models of educational equity at the school-district level. Five such models were funded. One of these cases is the three-year effort in Broward County, Florida, where teachers and administrators underwent various activities to develop gender awareness and to adopt materials for use in the classroom. The evaluation of this project showed that the school district gained a good understanding of sex-equity education and that new practices emerged in several classrooms, but that the project did not succeed in producing an exportable model (Bornstein 1985). This is not surprising, given the high degree of embeddedness that confronts efforts to redefine or abandon traditional practices.

To obtain WEEA funds states and school districts had to develop proposals and apply for funding, and — as noted earlier — most were not funded. Federal efforts in support of innovations in gender issues in education had been reduced in 1996 to the creation of a Gender Equity Expert Panel (with minimal funding) under the Office of Educational Research and Improvement (an office of the U.S. Department of Education), whose purpose it is to identify, review and recommend promising and exemplary programs, products, and practices to educators and community members concerned with working on gender in education. By 1997 it was uncertain that the panel's work would continue in the absence of federal support.

It is of interest to observe that while the progressive Clinton administration (1992–present) has not taken steps against the educational legislation on gender (unlike the Reagan and Bush administrations), it has not been able to alter the tide against it, which has come essentially as a product of drastic reductions in the government budget.

Achievements and Attributions

Implementation is crucial to turn words and intentions stated in public policy into a reality. Surprisingly, no major national evaluation exists to date of either Title-IX or WEEA, and studies of their implementation are very scarce. They can be found mostly in doctoral dissertations, not in studies by more established researchers. A few articles have appeared in scholarly journals or as book chapters (see, for instance, Stromquist 1993, 1997a and b). It is difficult to attribute solely to gender-equity legislation much of the observable outcomes because several other factors were at work during its existence, notably the women's movements and changes in the economy that have made it necessary for women to join the labor market. Nonetheless, the implementation of Title-IX and WEEA have some features that can be linked to the perceived outcomes. Putting together the fragmented literature produces the following picture.

Compliance with Title-IX Requirements

Most school districts achieved partial compliance of Title-IX inasmuch as they gave assurances to OCR of non-discrimination, appointed a Title-IX co-ordinator, and notified others that they did not discriminate on the basis of sex. Most also made courses that had been gender-segregated open to both girls and boys (e.g., home economics, automechanics, wood shop, and metal shop). A smaller number of districts seem to have developed internal grievance procedures, conducted a self-evaluation of their treatment of men and women, and provided comparable facilities and equipment in sports (Sanborn 1983; Florencio 1979).[4] It appears that very few states were able to provide technical assistance to school districts or to check compliance regulations against district procedures (Sanborn 1983). In part, this was due to lack of funds, since Title-IX did not provide any financial resources to enable educational institutions to move into full compliance. An area where lack of funds became important concerned sports equipment and facilities.

In the early years of the law's existence, Title-IX co-ordinators tended to be mostly male administrators — reflecting the overall low representation of women as administrators. While this has changed somewhat, Title-IX co-ordinators have tended to be persons with other, primary assignments (ranging from superintendent to accountant), with the consequence that Title-IX obligations are often slighted. A study of Iowa public school districts, based on a sample of 10 percent, found that 46 percent of these co-ordinators felt uncomfortable or neutral with their assignments (Florencio 1979). The limited commitment to Title-IX on the part of its local enforcers was corroborated in a study by Smith (1978), who found that principals and district-level administrators tended to have only a "superficial knowledge of the concerns" addressed in Title-IX. The study by Florencio found that while the role of the co-ordinator was not very well-defined, large school districts had fewer violations than middle-sized and small school districts in areas such as hiring women administrators and providing more balanced allocations to boys' and girls' athletics.

One of the few official evaluations of Title-IX at the national level was conducted in 1993. This study, based on survey data, found that sex discrimination had been eliminated from policies and programs but problems remained in drop-outs, in gender bias in student/teacher interactions, in participation and achievement of girls in math and science, in enrolment in and completion of vocational education courses in historically non-traditional fields for girls and boys, in teenage pregnancy and parenting, and in sexual harassment (The Mid-Atlantic Equity Consortium and The Network, 1993).[5] The study found that, although girls dropped out at rates slightly lower than boys, they were less likely to return to school or to obtain a GED, a certificate equivalent to high school education which can be obtained through a special exam (42 percent return for boys in contrast to 23 percent for girls). Hispanic and Afro-American men were found to return to school at a rate 10 percent higher than that of women of these ethnic groups. Among young women, pregnancy appeared as the major reason for dropping out of school in 44 percent of the cases.

An evaluation of the impact of Title-IX during 1975–1990 in the state of New York concluded that the number of women in higher and professional education had increased but that sexual harassment, a glass ceiling, and an overrepresentation of women in traditionally female professions were prevalent. It also noted that women were earning lower pay than men with less education and that there were fewer women than men in tenured jobs in the university. This evaluation did not attempt to link the various findings to possible effects of Title-IX (Burke, 1993).

Several of the feminist and gender-sensitive groups that lobbied for the development of gender-equity policies in education have continued to monitor the implementation of this legislation. Some important groups such as PEER (Project on Equal Education Rights) no longer exist due to lack of funding. The National Coalition for Women and Girls in Education, a major umbrella group representing such organizations as the American Association of University Women (which was extremely active in the passing of WEEA), the Women's Education Action League, the National Coalition for Sex Equity in Education, the Women's Sports Foundation, and the American Federation of Teachers, continues its lobbying efforts. In these days of economic constraints and "budget balancing," it is not certain whether these interest groups will succeed in securing renewed funding for WEEA.

Access of Girls and Women to Courses and Fields of Study

As in most other industrialized countries, the gender "problem" regarding schooling was not in access to primary and secondary schooling but in the sex-segregated nature of participation in certain high school courses and academic fields at the university level. The legislation to address gender inequalities, of course, recognizes that the participation of women and men in these courses and disciplines is not simply a question of individual preference but that it is the result of socialization messages and experiences inside and outside the schools that ultimately led to those "choices."

Since the enactment of Title-IX and WEEA, progress has occurred in the participation of women in a number of fields At the secondary school level, courses that differentiated by sex became open to boys and girls. Home economics and typing used to be accessible only to girls, and industrial arts and vocational education were open mostly to boys. At present, one finds a visibly reduced gender segregation, but since participation in these courses is mostly voluntary, an imbalance in certain courses continues.

In higher education today, a much larger representation of women students than in 1960 can be found across many fields, particularly law and medicine, where women in 1986 represented 40 and 31 percent of the enrollment, in contrast with 7 and 9 percent, respectively, in 1972. Women's participation in traditionally feminine fields, such as education and foreign languages, has not changed at all over the same period. Engineering reported gains, moving from about 1 percent in 1972 to over 10 percent in 1986 (American Council on Education 1989).

A study of the women's enrolment growth between 1960 and 1980 in most of the professions involved a survey sent to the deans of all professional schools in existence in 1960 in order to determine their views of the factors promoting these changes. According to these persons, the most important factors — in descending order — had been the increased number of women applicants (as opposed to policy changes in admissions), increased cultural acceptance of female professionals, positive social sanctions, female student role models, positive media portrayal, and acceptance by male peers and faculty. Legislative mandates such as the Civil Rights Act and Title-IX were considered by the deans to have had "negligible influence" (Wheeler-Mehan 1983). The changes, according to the deans, seem to have been more due to societal attitudes than to legislative force.

Participation of Girls and Women in Sports

Changes in the field of athletics have been considerable, even though athletics has been the most contested areas of the gender equity legislation. "In 1972, the average college spent less than 2 cents of every dollar of its athletic budget on women's sports. By 1980, the average had risen to 16.4 cent" (Macy 1996, p. 136)

Special growth has occurred in women's basketball, gymnastics, track, and swimming. By 1994 61 percent of the girls participated in interscholastic sports and and 56 percent in intercollegiate athletics programs, up from 7 and 15 percent, respectively, in 1971–1974. However, the average percentage of the college athletic budget assigned to women's sports was 26 percent in 1994 (U.S. Congress 1995).

The improvement in girls' sports continues to be heavily contested. Hearings of Title-IX conducted by the House of Representatives in 1995 concentrated exclusively on the athletics provision, in response to complaints by sports associations and coaches from several educational institutions that boys' sports were "being threatened by the increasing attention to girls' sports" (U.S. Congress 1995).

Gender-Sensitive Textbooks and Curricula

On the question of textbooks, the evidence seems to indicate that significant changes have occurred in primary and secondary education, but much less so at the university level. Though not within the purview of Title-IX, some of the largest textbook publishing houses have removed sexual stereotypes and bias from their books. Shakeshaft (1986), writing almost fifteen years after the enactment of Title-IX, reported on the uneven treatment of males and females in school textbooks, including the invisibility of female characters and the use of male-only language. A more recent study, by Sleeter and Grant (1991), based on a large sample of textbooks, reported that whites dominated the story lines in most textbooks and that women and people of color were assigned a much more limited range of roles than white males. Another review of textbooks, this time of California textbooks, showed subtle language bias, neglect of scholarship of women, omission of women as developers of history and initiators of events, and absence of women from accounts of technological developments (AAUW 1992).

Evidence from textbooks utilized in higher education presents a rather negative picture. A study by Sadker and Sadker (1980) reviewed 24 of the most popular textbooks used in pre-service teacher training programs during 1973–1978. Their content analysis of these textbooks revealed that discussion of sexism occupied less than 1 percent of the narrative, that sex equity tended to be omitted entirely or given incomplete treatment, and that, although there are many women educators, their contributions to education were not even mentioned. Sadker and Sadker also discovered that science and math textbooks — subject areas in which women tend to be considerably less prominent — showed the greatest imbalance in the treatment of boys and girls.

Another study of higher education materials is that conducted by Reid (1981), who examined the five most widely used introductory books in educational administration published between 1972 and 1977 for future elementary and secondary school principals, which the author estimated would influence over 10,000 newly certified school principals each year. The textbooks were analyzed in terms of narrative content, research framework, language, and illustrations. They were found to contain widespread sex bias and to devote a miniscule amount of content to such issues as treatment of sexism and efforts to redress it (Reid 1981). This study, it must be noted, covered a period shortly after the enactment of Title-IX and thus may not have reflected new gender sensitivity.

Further reflecting that perhaps societal influences are more responsible for the changes in the educational system than the law itself is the change that has occurred in textbooks, even though these were specifically left out of the legislation. Textbooks in primary and secondary education seem to have undergone the most significant changes, even though they are still far from being totally gender-sensitive.

Federal government officials have indicated at times that the government is committed to improving the participation of girls and women in science and technology, and often invoke the existence of the Eisenhower Math and Science Educational Act (of 1984) as the main mechanism. This Act seeks the improvement of science and technology in primary and secondary schools. It has received increasing funding, reaching about $280 million in 1993. The Eisenhower Act, however, funds a broad reform of math and science curricula, but with no specific reference to women. An evaluation by SRI in 1988–1989 found that less than 25 percent of the Eisenhower fund recipients had made service to "under-represented and under-served populations" an explicit component of their activities.

The Nature of the State

While there exists a variety of feminist perspectives on the state, with some attributing to it more benevolent and responsive roles, I wish to explore the position that considers the state the main manager of the power relations of gender. According to this view, the state shapes gender relations through rules of divorce, marriage, abortion, wages, sexuality, masculinized hierarchy, property, and the organization of collective violence (Walby 1990; Pateman 1988; Connell 1989). The state is male-centered through the sexual division of labor that places mostly men in the leadership of the state, in the way the bureaucracy has developed, and in the conceptualization of policies that frame women as recipients of the state's goodwill rather than as actors in the reshaping of the social relations of gender.

The patriarchal nature of the state, however, is not static. Voting rights for women were gained through a long struggle by the women's movement. In several other countries, it occurred through an imitation process. This indicates that as certain conditions are accepted in a country, a process of international contagion — or isomorphism — ensues. Economic forces also contribute: enabling the full participation of women in the labor force, dominant forces have modernized gender all over the world. At the same time, the state has neutralized feminist demands through concessions that do not eliminate fundamental obstacles to women's equality (Connell 1989; Stromquist 1997a). For example, one of the state responses in the domain of schooling is to recognize the principle of equal opportunity, rather than the need for anti-sexist education (Kelly 1988; Yates 1993).

The fact that states, regardless of their degree of overall democratization, continue to keep women in disadvantage is obvious from an examination of the socioeconomic indicators developed by the United Nations Development Program. Important measures in this context are the Human Development Index (HDI), the Gender Development Index (GDI), and the Gender Empowerment Measure (GEM) (UNDP 1995).[6] All these measures have been calibrated so that the maximum score is 1.0. The GDI reveals that the welfare of the citizens in general tends to be higher than that specifically of women in every country. The gender differentials can be slight in the case of Scandinavian countries (about 2 percentage points) or greater in the case the least developed countries (UNDP, 1996, pp. 135–137 and 138–140).

When it comes to measuring more precisely the amount of economic and political power, even in the best of cases (the Scandinavian countries again), women's power is only 75 percent that of men. And in the 84 percent of the countries for which the GEM indicator can be computed (as the data required are not available in the others), the GEM indicates that women have less than half the power of men (UNDP 1995, pp. 84–5). The United States ranks among the top five countries in terms of the HDI and GDI, but falls to eighth position in terms of the GEM. Two features characterize the United States: its very strong industrial development and its active women's movement. The latter is widely recognized as one of the largest and most active women's movements in the world.

A significant achievement of the UN Decade on Women (1976–1985) was to convince international development agencies and, concomitantly, national governments to include women in national development plans. For its part, the women's movement over time has become more eager to face issues of public power. Today, therefore, the feminist agenda places a greater emphasis on politics and political institutions (Tinker 1990). On the question of gender, governments have in recent years set up machineries within their public bureaucracies (Women in Development, or WID, units) to attend to issues regarding the condition and status of women. These units operate in many countries, but by and large they are understaffed, have access to miniscule budgets, and face mandates whose tasks greatly exceed the WID units' resources (Goetz 1995; Stromquist 1998).

By claiming legitimacy on the basis of individual citizenship, states make themselves vulnerable to demands of inclusion from marginalized groups. Claims of equality along diverse lines of race and sex touch at the core of states that depict themselves as just and democratic. A response to such demands, therefore, may be postponed but not totally ignored. At the same time, it is likely that this response will not be implemented by the state in a way that completely satisfies the group(s) making the demand because such accommodation may result in weaker control by the state or, at a minimum, represent a period of transition with many unknowns.

There is cross-national evidence that states are more likely to engage in coercive policies that mandate the elimination of discrimination than in supportive policies that promote system change (through the devolution of authority and creation of new political institutions and agencies) or in constructive policies (that promote new behaviors, knowledge, and attitudes regarding women and men in society) (Stromquist 1997a). That coercive policies are much more popular can be explained by the smaller financial requirements they present in contrast to those of supportive and constructive policies, but an even greater reason for their predominance is that they represent incremental and slight changes to the gender system.

In tracing the trajectory of gender-based legislation in the United States, the federal response appears at first face as very progressive, since it promoted both coercive legislation (Title-IX) and constructive legislation (WEEA). On deeper analysis, however, subsequent alterations and modifications severely weakened both, especially the more expensive and potentially influential one, WEEA.

Title-IX did not cover core issues regarding the educational experience, such as textbook and course content and the practices of teachers. While it prohibited discrimination, it did not offer funds to facilitate compliance and the agency assigned to enforce it (OCR) was by most accounts understaffed. The state, in the form of the courts and to some extent Congress, questioned key aspects of Title-IX, rendering it very ineffectual. Through the federal legislature, the state drastically reduced the support of WEEA, making it unable to meet its original objectives. Cleverly, the reduction was gradual — not dramatic. However, the state did not perform in a totally uniform manner, thus showing the contradictions inherent in a system that adheres simultaneously to patriarchal and democratic principles. Portions of the state in combination with civil society were able to rescue the initial meaning of the Title-IX legislation, namely its application to the entire institution not just to the program receiving federal funds. This was accomplished through the Civil Rights Restoration Act of 1988.

The initial weak performance of education officials at the state and school district level indicates that the public bureaucracy also functioned, at the level of individual administrators, to implement Title-IX in ways that were both weak and incomplete. Here, however, the notion of state and society becomes fuzzy, because reluctant bureaucrats were behaving, on the one hand, as state representatives protecting the current gender status quo, but on the other hand, they were also enacting their own gender beliefs that sex discrimination was really minimal and was exceeded by several other types of educational problems. The lack of training targeted for the Title-IX co-ordinators — those who were to monitor the implementation of Title-IX — appears from a policy design to have been a major flaw. From the perspective of the state as patriarchal and reluctant to engage in progressive sexual politics, the absence of training can be explained as a way to propose social change while simultaneously engaging in a minimum of transformation in the meaning of gender.

WEEA was a constructive policy, enabling educational institutions to move into new knowledge and behaviors. Yet, it was so poorly funded that its coverage was extremely limited. Moreover, WEEA relied on voluntary efforts: interested districts were to apply for funds to engage in innovative ways; those reluctant to change did not have to compete.

Conclusions

Through feminist initiative and pressure, two laws affecting education were passed with significant repercussions for the schooling of women at all levels. While the U.S. government enacted Title-IX and WEEA — laws that covered practically every educational institution and have been in existence for nearly twenty-five years — they were narrow in scope, received limited funding, and suffered from weak implementation. Moreover, these laws have not been reviewed to consider further improvement.[7]

The current political climate, with the U.S. Supreme Court's backing of Proposition 209 in California, not only questions the need for remedial action to ensure greater representation of racial minorities and women in the labor market and educational institutions, but it distorts the degree to which legislation has actively accomplished this representation. Further, the need to be sensitive to backlash against gender and race threatens to weaken the already fragile alliance between these groups.

The story of Title-IX and WEEA in the United States has not ended. While it is true that U.S. society "has a long history of using differences to establish and maintain hierarchies of power and privilege, with white males dominating virtually all other groups in educational, political, economic, and cultural domains" (Pollard 1992, p. 1), so far the Clinton administration, which owes women much in return for their share of the winning votes, has done little to support women's rights.

So far, however, the performance of the state concerning feminist demands demonstrates a willingness to act in the symbolic terrain: in opposition to sex discrimination as antithetical to the equal treatment of all individuals as equal citizens and members of the state, yet contradicted by concrete decisions restricting the effectiveness of sex-equity legislation, particularly its enforcement and funding. There have been instances that could be called bureaucratic incompetence such as OCR's sluggish responses to gender-based complaints or the inability of its staff to provide crucial technical assistance to a variety of educational institutions. But even this incompetence seems to be an issue that could have been averted had the state assigned greater importance to the gender problem.

Although educational legislation in favor of women was enacted by the federal government, the "state" we are discussing in connection to Title-IX and WEEA has vacillated between being hostile and mildly responsive. Sexual politics have been active in terms of acknowledging women's demands and interests. But they have also been present in framing the state response in a way that did not touch the ideological core of the state, that which is reflected in the content and practices of educational systems. Sexual politics became activated in the clear struggle to preserve norms of masculinity by upholding some sports as more worthy of support (funding) than others, by using the courts to question definitions that would affect the scope of Title-IX, and ultimately by claiming that success had been reached and that gender "problems" were limited to narrow (though not unimportant) issues such as the need to increase the numbers of girls and women in science and technology or to identify and implement existing educational programs that had been found to be "exemplary" or "promising".

Important unintended effects have been the changes brought about by the increased number of women in athletics. Through the steady entry of women into a wider range of sports, femininity and masculinity are being redefined along less binary lines. Girls today are participating in sports in which they would not have imagined themselves twenty years ago. This experience has been found, mostly anecdotally at present, to affect positively their sense of self-esteem as well as to make the space provided by sports a less male-centered arena. It is to be hoped that these feelings will translate into less conventional choices regarding occupation and life organization.

Educational institutions — inasmuch as people are there to learn — remain the settings with the greatest likelihood of engaging in an open debate about the democratization of gender relations. They cannot be left out of feminist demands for transformation. The state, as the main provider of schooling, must continue also to be the target of increased demands for educational policy formulation. The experience of the United States shows that democratic states respond to feminist claims, but without continued pressure measures soon fall into diluted forms of responsiveness.

Affirming the need to act upon the state, Connell argues that we need to act on a large scale to secure the creation of a new gender order. In his view, which I share, the "problem is not engagement in the arena of the state, but the shape of that engagement" (1989, p. 29). According to Connell, there is a need to reshape the state and replace its masculinized "core" of decision making and enforcement through demilitarization and participatory democracy. In this approach, the role of mass movements, particularly women-based non-governmental organizations, will be critical, not only to provide constant watch over state policies but to invent the type of democracy that is most sensitive to new forms of social arrangements.

Notes

1. To suggest that the feminist movement did not pay sufficient attention to primary and secondary formal education should not detract from its work in fulfilling crucial educational functions of a nonformal nature and in promoting important changes at the university level. This work included questioning the existence of patriarchal ideologies in society; developing feminist newspapers, magazines, journals, and publishing companies; establishing women's studies programs in numerous universities; and offering feminist critiques of several disciplines, particularly those in the social sciences.

2. This bill was endorsed by over 200 national organizations, including the Leadership Conference on Civil Rights, the National Association of Independent Colleges and Universities, and numerous religious organizations.

3. In 1996 support stopped not only for WEEA but also for Civil Rights Act Title IV state equity co-ordinators, who have been an important source of technical assistance to school districts in their actions against both racial and gender discrimination.

4. Sanborn's study, a doctoral dissertation, was based on a two-year effort that covered in-person interviews of state-level Title-IX co-ordinators in 46 states. The study also included interviews with several Title-IX co-ordinators at school-district level, staff members in OCR, and several feminist groups monitoring Title-IX.
5. This study, sponsored by the government, is rather brief and superficial.
6. The HDI combines three indicators (life expectancy at birth, adult literacy rate, and gross enrollment in education at all levels); the GDI compares HDI levels of women and men; and the GEM considers women's degree of decision making in economic and political life through such indicators as the proportion of women in parliamentary positions, as administrators and managers, and as professional and technical workers, and the women's proportion of earned income at the national level (UNDP, 1995).
7. Australia, in clear contrast with the United States, has moved into a third-generation law. After a study in 1975 that framed many policy decisions, it enacted the National Policy on the Education of Girls (Tsolidis 1996). This was followed by the National Action Plan for the Education of girls 1993–1997, a policy designed as a "practical addition" to the National Policy, but which also reflected new research and a broader conceptual framework. According to Tsolidis, the Action Plan emphasizes the social construction of gender and highlights and even challenges the role of schooling in this process through the formation of femininity and masculinity.

References

American Association of University Women. 1992. *How Schools Shortchange Girls: A Study of Major Findings on Girls and Education.* Washington, D.C.: AAUW.

American Council on Education. 1989. *1989-90 Fact Book on Higher Education.* New York: ACE.

Applied Systems Institute. 1985. *A Descriptive Analysis of the Women's Educational Equity Program.* Washington, D.C.: ASI.

Bornstein, Rita. 1985. 'Ambiguity as Opportunity and Constraint: Evaluation of a Federal Sex Equity Education Program'. *Educational Evaluation and Policy Analysis* 7[2]: 99–114.

Brown, Cynthia, and Jill Reid. 1987. *Twenty Years on: New Federal and State Roles to Achieve Equity in Education.* Washington, D.C.: National Center for Policy Alternatives.

Burke, Geraldine. 1993. *Equity for Women in the 1990s: Regents Policy and Action Plan with Supporting Background*. Albany: University of the State of New York and the State Department of Education.

Connell, Robert. 1989. *The State in Sexual Politics: Theory and Appraisal*. Sydney: Macquarie University, mimeo.

The Editors, Harvard Educational Review. 1979. An Interview on Title-IX with Shirley Chisholm, Holly Knox, Leslie R. Wolfe, Cynthia G. Brown, and Mary Kaaren Jolly. *Harvard Educational Review* 49(1): 514–526.

Florencio, George. 1979. *A Study of Compliance with Title-IX of the Education Amendments of 1972 in Selected Iowa Public School Districts*. Des Moines: Ed.D. dissertation, Drake University.

Goetz, Anne Marie. 1995. *The Politics of Integrating Gender to State Development Processes*. Geneva: UN Research Institute for Social Development.

Kelly, Gail. 1988. *Liberating Women's Education from Development: A Critique of the Women in Development Literature*. Buffalo: State University of New York at Buffalo, mimeo.

Macy, S. 1996. *Winning Ways*. New York: Henry Holt.

The Mid-Atlantic Equity Consortium and The Network. 1993. *Beyond Title-IX: Gender Equity Issues in the Schools*. Chevy Chase, Maryland: The Mid-Atlantic Equity Consortium and The Network.

Office for Civil Rights. 1991. *Annual Report to Congress. Fiscal Year 1990*. Washington, D.C.: Office for Civil Rights, U.S.Department of Education.

Pateman, Carol. 1988. *The Sexual Contract*. Stanford: Stanford University Press.

Pollard, Diane S. and Avery, Maria-Paz Beltran. 1992. 'Toward a Pluralistic Perspective on Equity'. *Women's Educational Equity Act Publishing Center Digest*. February: 1–8.

Reid, Beverly. 1981. *Content Analysis of Sexism in Educational Administration Textbooks*. Washington, D.C.: Ed.D. dissertation, The American University.

Sadker, Myra, and David Sadker. 1980. 'Sexism in teacher-education texts'. *Harvard Educational Review* 50(1): 36–46.

Sanborn, Virginia. 1983. *A National Study of Title-IX and Its Impact upon Public Education 1975–1980*. Los Angeles: Ph.D. dissertation, University of Southern California.

Shakeshaft, Carol. 1986. 'A gender at risk'. *Phi Delta Kappa* 67(7): 499–503.

Sleeter, Christine, and Carl Grant. 1991. Race, class, gender, and disability in current textbooks. In Michael Apple and Linda Christian-Smith, eds., *The Politics of the Textbook*. New York: Routledge and Chapman Hall.

Smith, Ann Dolores. 1978. *Secondary School Programs and Title-IX Legislation: Perceptions of Selected Secondary School Principals in Illinois*. Carbondale: Ph.D. dissertation, Southern Illinois University.

Stromquist, Nelly. 1993. Sex-equity legislation in education: The state as promoter of women's rights. *Review of Educational Research* 63(4): 379–407.

Stromquist, Nelly. 1997a. State policies and gender equity: Comparative perspectives. In Barbara Bank and Peter Hall, eds. *Gender, Equity, and Schooling: Policy and Practice.* New York: Garland Publishing.

Stromquist, Nelly. 1997b. Gender policies in American education: Reflections on federal legislation and action. In Catherine Marshall, ed., *Comparative Education Legislation on Gender.* Hampshire, U.K: Falmer Press.

Stromquist, Nelly. 1998. 'The institutionalization of gender and its impact on educational policy'. *Comparative Education* 34(1) (forthcoming).

Tinker, Irene. 1990. The making of a field: Advocates, practitioners, and scholars. In Irene Tinker, ed., *Persistent Inequalities. Women and World Development.* New York: Oxford University Press, 27–53.

Tsolidis, Georgina. 1996. Feminist theorization of identity and difference: A case study related to gender education policy. *British Journal of Sociology of Education* 17(3): 267–77.

United Nations. 1995. *Human Development Report 1995.* New York: UNDP.

U.S. Congress. 1995. *Hearing on Title-IX of the Education Amendments of 1972. Hearing before the Subcommittee on Postsecondary Education, Training, and Life-long Learning of the Committee on Economic and Educational Opportunities, House of Representatives, 104th Congress, First Session.* Washington, D.C.: Government Printing Office.

Walby, Sylvia. 1990. *Theorizing Patriarchy.* Oxford: Basil Blackwell.

Wheeler-Mehan, Linda. 1983. *Analysis of Factors Related to the Increase of Women Graduates from Professional Schools in the United States from 1960 through 1980.* Malibu: Ed.D. dissertation, Pepperdine University.

Yates, Lyn. 1993. 'Feminism and Australian state policy. Some questions for the 1990s'. In Madeleine Arnot and Kathleen Weiler, eds., *Feminism and Social Justice in Education: International Perspectives.* London: Falmer Press.

CHAPTER 6

"Doing Gender" in Canadian Schools: An Overview of the Policy and Practice Mélange

Rebecca Priegert Coulter

For nearly thirty years in Canada, the federal, provincial, and territorial governments[1] have generated policy directives on women and education in an intermittent, piecemeal fashion and the response in schools has varied from hostile resistance through casual disregard to partial compliance and tentative acceptance. As a result, different configurations of the policy-practice nexus can be discerned in the four public policy domains that have dominated the field of what Canadians now call "gender equity in education." While the four domains clearly overlap, they are distinct enough to be considered separately. The first domain takes as its content questions of curriculum and pedagogy with the early focus on sex-role stereotyping now giving way to an interest in anti-sexist education and the inclusive curriculum. A second set of interests grows from the question of girls in mathematics, science and technology. A third grouping of policy-practice questions centres on violence against women in schools. The fourth set of concerns revolves around women in positions of educational leadership.

In each of these four policy domains, efforts to move beyond the separate worlds of policy and practice to a world of policy with practice have been largely driven by teachers working individually, in small groups or larger networks, or through teacher federations, and often in conjunction with sympathetic women, those whom Eisenstein (1991) calls "femocrats," in ministries of education and women's secretariats. The possibilities for action have been variously enhanced or constrained by specific sets of circumstances and social contexts, including the availability of resources, the impact of free-trade agreements, and the nature of dominant discourses about equality, individual rights, the free market and globalization (Coulter forthcoming). Indeed, an analysis of achievements and setbacks in each of the four policy domains illustrates how gender equity work in education in Canada does not exist in isolation from wider concerns in the polity and economy.

The Curriculum and Pedagogical Practices

It is safe to say that a major emphasis in work on gender and education for the last thirty years has been in the area of curriculum and pedagogy and on students' experiences of schooling (Coulter 1996a). By the late 1960s, the Canadian women's movement had identified sex-role stereotyping as the key issue facing girls in school and this analysis was reinforced in the *Report of the Royal Commission on the Status of Women* (1970), which recommended that provincial governments "adopt textbooks that portray women, as well as men, in diversified roles and occupations" (p. 175). Over the next five years, several reports on bias in textbooks appeared across the country and provincial governments responded by introducing policy guidelines designed to eliminate sex-role stereotyping in classroom materials (Julien 1987). In Ontario, for example, textbook evaluators were told to assess materials for sex bias in the areas of language use, the selection of illustrations and the portrayal of male and female roles, personality characteristics, abilities and self-concepts. Texts for literature and history courses were expected to display a "reasonable" balance of male and female characters (Ontario Ministry of Education 1988).

In Canada, as elsewhere, the 1970s were years when women's issues were garnering a great deal of media attention and the women's movement was very active. Feminist organizing around International Women's Year in 1975 generated much discussion about women's inequality and many provincial governments responded through their Ministries of Education by developing broad policy statements about sex equity. Ontario provides a strong example of this development. In 1975 a new programme of studies for elementary schools was issued. It noted that all children should be able to "develop abilities and aspirations without the limitations imposed by sex role stereotypes" (Ontario Ministry of Education, 1975 p. 4). By the mid-1980s, each secondary school in Ontario was instructed to ensure that the philosophy of sex equity permeated "all aspects of the school's curriculum, policies, teaching methods and materials, and assessment procedures, as well as the attitudes and expectations of its staff" (Ontario Ministry of Education 1989, p. 11). A survey conducted for the Council of Ministers of Education in 1987 was told that in Ontario "all curriculum documents, policy circulars, guidelines, and resource and support documents, since the mid-1970s, have been written or revised to reflect the Ministry's growing commitment to the philosophy of sex equity" (Julien 1987, p. 23).

During the 1970s, as well, attention was given to producing resources that would give women a presence in the curriculum. For example, Ministries of Education in British Columbia and Ontario produced resource guides on women's studies which included sample units, reference lists and teaching ideas. Teacher federations in several provinces developed a wide range of curriculum kits and packages on topics such as famous Canadian women, pioneer women, and women at work. More recently, individual school boards have begun to provide curriculum documents and materials for classroom use. This "add women and stir" approach to curriculum revision persists to this day. By the early 1980s, the self-esteem movement had gained momentum, too, and the education system witnessed the growth of a range of strategies designed to improve the ways in which girls perceived themselves. Career days for girls, role modelling programmes and workshops on body image were offered in school jurisdictions across Canada.

Tokenism in the curriculum and self-esteem projects are both based on the notion that sex-role socialization is "the problem" and information about women's contributions and potentials will convince girls to look beyond marriage and motherhood to paid employment and work in non-traditional occupations. This explanatory framework and the form it takes in practice have become ubiquitous. The Maritime Provinces Education Foundation proclaimed in 1991 that the gender problem in education could be resolved by improving girls' self-image, exposing them to a wider range of career options and providing role models, thus simply reiterating the old and uncritical wisdom that had been around for more than two decades. Ontario's recent Royal Commission on Learning (1994) adopted a similar view when it identified sex-role stereotyping and the lack of women's awareness of career options as the key gender issues in education.

However, as Gaskell, McLaren, and Novogrodsky (1989) argue, policies and practices based on a sex-role analysis and role-modelling programmes are clearly inadequate, for they "leave unchallenged the gender bias in schools...[and are built] on the assumption that girls must be changed. Men are the model of achievement, and compared to men, women don't measure up" (p. 16). In other words, the emphasis on changing individual girls, on making them less "defective boys," effectively ignores the systemic nature of sexism in schools. Systemic issues have been taken up more actively in the anti-sexist approaches evident in some recent policy documents and in some school board programmes. In 1994, the Ontario Ministry of Education and Training circulated a validation draft of a support document for teachers called Engendering Equity. This document called for a transformed and inclusive curriculum that would require the "causes and patterns of sexism, racism, and all forms of discrimination and prejudice" to be "explored and challenged" in schools (p. 4). In 1991, the Toronto Board of Education established a four-day parallel retreat programme for secondary school students. Each year two groups of forty young women and forty young men meet separately for three days to discuss sexism, sexuality, homophobia, and violence. On the fourth day the two groups meet together to share ideas and strategies for change. The purpose of the retreat programme is to help both teachers and students "begin to understand some difficult concepts: One is that sexism is a form of systemic discrimination which ensures the power of one group in society over another group. Sexism isn't just what individuals say or do, it relates to the entire way we've set up a male-dominated society. The second is the perplexing idea that patriarchy is a system not only of oppression of women, but one that has a contradictory impact on men as well: men's privileges and power are linked to the pain and alienation suffered by men themselves" (Novogrodsky et al. 1992, pp. 69–70).

Organizers of the four-day retreat create a context which situates gender in relation to class, race, ethnicity, and sexual orientation, emphasizes women's agency and ability to effect change, and defuses feelings of guilt among the young men in order to allow them to see ways they might support women in challenging the sexist nature of society. Admittedly, explicit anti-sexist teaching is still rare in Canada when compared to the more traditional approach of token units, add-on materials, role modelling programmes and self-esteem workshops. Indeed, with the election of governments committed to a neo-liberal economic agenda and, increasingly, a neo-conservative social agenda, the struggle for anti-sexist polices and practices will become even more difficult. The support document mentioned above, Engendering Equity (Ontario Ministry of Education and Training 1994) was developed under a social democratic government, but before it could be finalized and officially distributed to schools, a new Progressive Conservative government was elected in Ontario and the document was withdrawn. The centralization of curriculum control, the imposition of provincial and national testing programmes, the cutbacks in school funding, and decreased access to resources will all affect the ability of teachers to engage in gender-equity work (Coulter 1996b). Indeed, in Ontario at least, gender-equity policies are disappearing in favour of much watered-down statements on equality of opportunity. In the proposed new secondary school programme of studies scheduled for implementation in 1998, for example, no mention is even made' of gender.

To date, the real impact of policy statements and curriculum development projects on actual classroom practice has never been evaluated. A handful of studies on the efficacy of policy guidelines on textbook content suggest these policies have made little substantive difference. Batcher, Winter, and Wright (1987) analysed all the grades four to six reading series approved for use in Ontario's schools in 1986 and concluded, "Sex equity did not exist in readers in 1975 and it does not exist now" (p. 27). A detailed examination of secondary school history and contemporary studies textbooks, all of which had been evaluated under the Ontario Ministry's anti-bias guidelines and approved, found that not one of the sixty-six books genuinely met the requirements of the sex-equity policy. Women were mentioned in many of the books, but their contributions were trivialized or marginalized (Light, Staton, and Bourne 1989). Baldwin and Baldwin's (1992) survey of classroom textbooks in use across Canada concluded that material on women was "included almost as an aside or to satisfy provincial guidelines, which could safely be ignored by teachers without disruption of the 'important' themes" (p. 113).

A research study commissioned by the Ontario Teachers' Federation bluntly revealed the reality that, "the relationship between Ministry publications and classroom practice is unknown" (Stevenson 1992, p. 21). A non-rigorous sampling of a selected number of school boards led to the conclusion that most school boards have initiated some work on gender, and the large boards, especially in the metropolitan Toronto area, have comprehensive equity programmes. Nonetheless, despite Ministry policies and curriculum guidelines, despite the production of a wide range of curriculum materials and despite the activities of feminist teachers working through teacher federation "Status of Women Committees," school-board staff believed that "few teachers in their jurisdictions had been exposed to ideas about gender equity in education in any serious or systematic way" (Stevenson 1992, p. 22). Indeed, it was felt that many teachers and school administrators were either uninterested in or antagonistic towards work on gender and education, a view confirmed by the experiences of a group of first-year feminist teachers working in Ontario schools who found ignorance of existing policies to be endemic and hostility towards gender equity to be widespread among teachers and students (Coulter 1995).

Girls and Mathematics, Science and Technology

Although public policy support for gender-equity initiatives in schooling is generally on the decline as a result of the current political climate, one exception can be found. Efforts to encourage girls and women to seek careers in mathematics, science and technology have been sustained and even intensified, primarily because, as Barlow and Robertson (1994) put it, the issue has been framed "as an employer-and-profit problem rather than as a matter of equity" (p. 128). They wryly observe that school subjects such as politics (65 percent male) and child development (95 percent female) reflect a greater gender differentiation than chemistry, but receive virtually no attention from policymakers. Mathematics, science and technology, however, are seen as areas of import to the well-being of the economy and getting the best and the brightest into those fields is crucial to Canada's competitive position in the global marketplace. Many female teachers and others interested in women's education have mapped onto this discourse of global competitiveness and new economic realities as a central strategy to draw attention to other gender questions in schooling. Hence, the corporations, the state and women have joined forces in this policy domain although for quite different reasons.

A massive range of programmes funded by governments and by private industry have sprung up as a means to increase women's participation in the sciences. A virtual flood of role modelling and mentoring programmes, posters, video kits, workshop packages, and other educational materials are available in every province and territory and scholarships are offered to entice women to enter and remain in the sciences at the post-secondary level. Several school boards are experimenting with single-sex classes to encourage girls in mathematics, physics and chemistry. University students are called into service to visit high schools to extol the virtues of careers in science or to offer summer courses to demonstrate how exciting science can be. Increasingly, efforts are also aimed at improving the science competence of elementary school teachers, most of whom are women, through professional development activities.

Despite the concentration of resources in this specific policy domain, success has been limited. Although testing programmes show little significant difference in the achievement levels of girls and boys in school, women have continued to demonstrate a real reluctance to study sciences in secondary schools when those subjects become optional and women fail to enrol in large numbers in engineering and applied sciences at university. In 1991, only 13 percent of the undergraduate degrees in those fields were awarded to women. In mathematics and physical sciences, women earned only 29 percent of the undergraduate degrees although overall women received 56 percent of the total number of degrees awarded by Canadian universities (Human Resources Development Canada 1994). As a result of these statistics, which are taken to signal the failure of pro-active policies and programmes, a deeper analysis of women's apparent lack of interest in the sciences is emerging. The nature and structure of the science disciplines, the ways in which they are taught, and the hostile environments women face when entering a domain traditionally regarded by men as theirs, are slowly coming to be questioned. As Acker and Oatley (1993) pointed out after examining a wide range of Canadian programmes and research literature in the field, our understanding of gender and science and what educational interventions might be successful is deficient. They conclude that "there is a difference, one highly significant for prospects for change in practice, between what research so far has told us, and what we actually need to know" (p. 268).

Violence in the Schools

Violence against women and children has received considerable, though not sufficient, attention in Canada. The women's movement has made violence a major area for organizing and lobbying, the media have provided significant coverage, governments have offered funding for services, and a wide range of community organizations have developed programming and support agencies. In Ontario the Ministry of Education and Training includes a Violence Prevention Secretariat which has responsibility for family violence-prevention initiatives. Most Ontario school boards have in-school educational programmes on family violence for students. These often take the form of whole-school assemblies during which invited "experts" lecture students who then return to their classrooms to discuss what they have learned. Many schools boards also have been partners with social service agencies, police departments and women's shelters in wider community-based efforts to prevent violence against women and children.

After the massacre of fourteen women engineering students in Montreal on 6 December 1989, educators became particularly active in developing programmes to stop violence against women. The Canadian Teachers' Federation (1990) developed a resource for teachers called *Thumbs Down: A Classroom Response to Violence Towards Women.* The Federation of Women Teachers' Associations of Ontario (FWTAO) launched a province-wide campaign geared to developing an awareness of the abuse of women and children. Other teacher federations produce materials and run campaigns to counter violence against women and children and have co-operated with community agencies to distribute information and provide services. In some schools, teachers and students work together to sponsor the annual white ribbon campaign, a programme which originated with a group of pro-feminist males who promoted the idea that men opposed to violence against women should wear a white ribbon during the first week of December to symbolize their commitment. In a small handful of schools, male teachers work with male students to develop programmes aimed at helping young men understand violence against women and men's responsibilities to work for change.

Most recently, research on date rape (Mercer 1988; Popaleni 1991) and on sexual harassment (Larkin 1994) has broken the silence on forms of violence young women experience, often in the school setting, and several steps have been taken to provide remedies. For example, the Ontario Secondary School Teachers' Federation, the Ontario Women's Directorate and the Violence Prevention Secretariat of the Ministry of Education and Training (1995) co-operated to fund the preparation and circulation of a comprehensive educational resource, *The Joke's Over: Student to Student Sexual Harassment in Secondary Schools.* This kit takes a whole-school approach to sexual harassment and contains materials for board and school administrators, teachers, support staff, students, parents and families. And yet, at the same time, the growing concern in Canada about school violence has led to policies and practices which fail to recognize that "If societal violence is not gender-neutral, it is implausible to conclude that school violence would be" (Robertson 1993, p. 50). The ability to set violence against women in its own compartment and away from violence in general reveals a deeply flawed analysis and raises central questions about the real commitment of the education system.

It should be remembered, too, that female students are not the only ones to suffer from specific forms of gender violence in the schools. In their national study, King and Peart (1992) discovered that one out of five female secondary school teachers worried about being physically injured by students. A study by the Manitoba Teachers' Society (1990) found that 66 percent of female teachers reported experiencing physical abuse and sexual harassment by students compared to only 34 percent of the males. Robertson (1993) found that existing ministry, school board and teacher federation policies on sexual harassment demonstrate "a continuum of awareness of the nature and gravity of harassment, and a conflicted view of culpability and responsibility in the event of harassment" (p. 46). She also concluded that there is simply not enough evidence to speak authoritatively on the extent or nature of sexual harassment experienced by women teachers and no research to help us evaluate whether existing policies have successfully deterred sexual harassment. Similarly, we do not currently know how much education about violence against women actually occurs in schools, how it is delivered or received and whether it makes any difference in behaviours.

Women in Educational Leadership

Teachers, compared to other women workers in Canada, are paid well and enjoy excellent benefits and reasonable working conditions. After decades of struggle, during which most provincial teacher federations became strong and politically astute unions, women now entering the profession can expect that they will receive the same pay and benefits as men with the same qualifications and experience. Although there is a gendered pattern in teaching in that women dominate the ranks in elementary schools while men are somewhat in the majority in secondary schools, the trend in Canada is towards a female teaching force regardless of grade level. While there are some lingering concerns about women's loss of pensionable service when they take maternity or family leave to work part-time while raising children, and growing concerns that the relative loss of purchasing power and worsening conditions of employment over the last ten years coincidentally match the re-feminization of teaching since 1986 (Coulter 1996b; Robertson 1993), the major employment issue for female teachers as expressed through their organizations has been women's significant under-representation in positions of educational leadership. Although not all female teachers believe that this focus on administrative positions is well-taken and would prefer that resources be directed towards changing the curriculum and teaching practices, "women in leadership" has come to dominate the agenda as the women's issue for teachers.

At least part of the reason for this must lie with the fact that women's exclusion from positions of authority in education is so easily documented. In 1989–1990, for example, women comprised 63.9 percent of the Canadian teaching force[2] but only 20.6 percent of the school principals were female (Robertson 1993, p. 22). More recent statistics for the province of Ontario show that in 1995–1996 women made up 75.4 percent of the public elementary teaching force but only 5.2 percent of women held positions of added responsibility (PARs) as vice-principals or principals. Men, on the other hand, made up only 24.6 percent of the teaching force but 18.4 percent of them had PARs. Put another way, 1 out of 19 women had a PAR while 1 out of 4 men did. In the Roman Catholic system, 79.3 percent of the elementary school teachers were female and 1 out of 27 held a PAR, compared to 1 out of 4 men. Interestingly, in the public secondary schools of the province where 46.0 percent of the teachers are women, 1 out of 5 held a PAR, whereas 1 out of 4 men did. Female teachers make up 48.6 percent of the teaching force in Roman Catholic secondary schools. One out of 6 women and 1 out of 4 men have PARs. Of the public secondary school principals, 27.1 percent were female, while 24.1 percent of Roman Catholic secondary school principals were (FWTAO 1996). These kinds of figures, which are basically the same in every province, are taken as incontrovertible evidence that women experience discrimination when it comes to administrative appointments.

By 1988, all the provinces except Alberta and Prince Edward Island had voluntary affirmative-action or employment-equity programmes for women in administration (MacLeod 1988). The Ontario Ministry of Education, generally regarded as a leader in this context had, in fact, been promoting voluntary action since 1973; although ten years later, and after intense lobbying by the FWTAO and its local associations, only 22 percent of the public boards had actually developed any specific policies. In 1985 the Ministry began providing incentive funding to school boards but remained unsatisfied with the progress being made by local school boards towards the goal of 30 percent women in supervisory positions. Finally, in 1989, the Education Act was amended to give the Minister of Education the power to require school boards to implement a policy of affirmative action with respect to the employment and promotion of women. Chris Ward, the Liberal Minister of Education of the day, declared that he would exercise the power granted to him under the Act and also indicated that the new goal was 50 percent women in positions of leadership by the year 2000. Until 1995, a succession of ministers of education reiterated this commitment.

While the figures for Ontario cited above suggest that women are still under-represented in the ranks of educational administration, there is a discernible pattern of improvement which must be at least partly attributable to the successful implementation of employment-equity policies. Put another way, there are quantifiable data which suggest that in this domain we find policy with practice, at least by one measure. For example, between 1979–1980 and 1995–1996, the percentage of principals who were female in public elementary schools went from 7 percent to 37.6 percent and in public secondary schools from 2.9 percent to 27.1 percent. The most marked improvement occurs in the period after the Minister made employment equity mandatory in 1989. Statistics for the Roman Catholic system are only available for the period 1986–1987 to 1995–1996, but they indicate that during that ten-year period in elementary schools, the percentage of principals who were female increased from 22.1 percent to 35.8 percent. In Roman Catholic secondary schools the percentage of female principals actually declined from 23.8 percent in 1986–1987 to 16.8 percent in 1991–1992 but then began to climb to 24.1 percent in 1995–1996 (FWTAO 1996). The period of women's declining representation was one of considerable and rapid growth in the system as a result of the extended funding granted by the province to the Catholic secondary system, but why this should affect women's access, albeit temporarily, to administration is not clear.

In 1995, an aggressively right-wing Conservative government was elected in Ontario. One of its first actions was to excise any reference to employment equity in provincial legislation, including the Education Act. As they were no longer required to engage in measures to correct imbalances in their workforces, school boards were ordered to destroy the employee information they had collected as part of the employment-equity implementation process. The destruction of employment-equity programmes has also meant that in many boards, employment-equity officers, most of whom were women, have lost their jobs or been redeployed. Because equity officers were often also responsible for educational-equity initiatives with respect to the curriculum, the loss of this personnel will inevitably affect the efforts of many boards to develop and implement policies on gender and education directed towards students. It is ironic that Ontario is moving from a period where there was arguably more policy than practice to a period where there will be more practice than policy because individual teachers, status-of-women committees in teacher organizations, and groups such as Educators for Gender Equity (Coulter 1996a) will continue to struggle with questions of gender and education.

Conclusion

This general review of gender-equity policies and practices in Canadian education has revealed a very uneven development of approaches, a veritable ragbag of differing understandings of problems and solutions. While it is possible to examine formal policies revealed in legislation, regulations, programmes of study, curriculum guidelines, collective agreements, administrative manuals and the like, it is virtually impossible to determine the extent to which practice bears any resemblance to policy. Even when we can document specific types of practices, the dearth of research means that there is no way of telling whether gender reform initiatives in the schools have made any difference and if they have, in what ways. Evaluation of programmes and practices is made even more difficult in Canada because of the country's size and diversity, because education is a provincial matter, and because provincial governments have, for the most part, allowed a considerable degree of local control over curriculum, pedagogy, and other aspects of schooling. Hence, even between two geographically coterminous school boards, vast differences might exist. Between well-resourced, urban, progressive boards and poor, isolated, socially conservative boards, the chasm can be enormous.

One way to evaluate the degree to which nearly thirty years of gender work in schools has been successful is to listen to the voices of female students. The nine- to twelve-year-olds who belong to the Young Women's Club at an inner-city elementary school in Toronto told Naveau (1992), "Everybody knows the boys get a lot more of everything in school — more money, more sports, more time for activities — since kindergarten!" (p. 86). A nine-year-old observed, "For sure boys and girls are not treated equally in school. Everybody knows that the boys get all the attention in class because they are so loud and so bad. They talk and talk and the teacher has to listen to them" (p. 86). "Everybody" may know, but other research indicates that 94 percent of young women and 93 percent of young men agree that both sexes have an equal opportunity to succeed in school (Holmes and Silverman 1992). Young women can describe their individual experiences of sexism and discrimination when asked to do so, young men can identify the ways in which they insult, intimidate, and control their female peers, and both groups easily provide examples of the ways in which teachers are sexist.[3] However, neither group seems to see the connection between these experiences and the question of equality of opportunity in schools. This may well be because when all is said and done, girls usually outperform boys in reading and writing and equal them in mathematics and science. From the perspective of the main mandate of schooling — academic achievement — young people see no equality issue. Yet the national study of teenagers conducted by Bibby and Posterski (1992) revealed that young women "continue to feel significantly inferior to young males when it comes to general competence" (pp. 146–7). There is an interesting set of complexities here which requires further exploration, at least partially because they suggest a less-than-adequate fit between policies and practices.

Teachers engaged in gender-equity work also are able to identify significant concerns about the problem of practice. Focus groups with Ontario teachers engaged in gender-equity work revealed common themes. The failure of teacher education programmes, whether pre-service or in-service, to address equity is seen as one difficulty. Another is the "serious lack of systematic data on the best methods of achieving gender awareness and developing skills for gender equity among teachers" (Ontario Teachers' Federation and Ontario Women's Directorate [OTF/OWD] 1994, p. 9). "One-off" professional development days are regarded as ineffective and of little or no value. Teachers feel it is unrealistic to assume that deeply embedded ideas and values can be dealt with in one day. Teachers "doing gender" feel isolated from one another and often indicate they lacked support from their administrators at the school and board levels. They experience various degrees of resistance and backlash to gender-equity initiatives from both colleagues and students. Too few resources for equity teaching and limited access to the few resources which exist are also issues. The materials which are available are too often single-issue kits, videos, or lesson plans and focus on non-controversial topics such as girls in non-traditional occupations or bias in the media. Materials and approaches which address power and privilege are essentially nonexistent and unlikely to appear any time soon (OTF/OWD, 1994).

Doing gender-equity work in the schools has never been easy. Today, achievements can be measured in the patchwork pattern of policies and in fragmented and inconsistent practices relying heavily on the time, energy and commitment of a small band of teachers working for social justice in their own locales, supported only sporadically by school administrators, teacher federations, ministry and school board femocrats and feminist activists. However empty the glass might seem, it is nonetheless also important to remember it is not empty, either. Young people are more aware than ever regarding gender issues. Polls indicate that the majority of Canadians, especially the young, support the broad goals of the women's movement. Young women have high expectations for themselves and for women in general, even as they see and understand some of the harsh realities of violence and the "double day" (Holmes and Silverman 1992). It is not implausible to assume that schooling has made some contribution to enhanced awareness and increased expectations among young women, as well as to some measure of understanding among young men. Teachers may feel isolated, unsupported, and lacking in education about gender, but they nonetheless manage to prepare new materials, scrounge resources, teach other teachers, and organize professional networks (Coulter 1996a). While confronting their day-to-day struggles, teachers easily forget the bigger picture and the gains which have been made over the long term.

Admittedly, the current attacks on public education and on teachers in Canada by right-wing governments (Barlow and Robertson 1994; Robertson and Smaller 1996), and the denial by those governments that equity is even an issue, put important gains at risk. Indeed, the disappearance of important policies on gender from the programmes of studies in some provinces places teachers doing gender-equity work in the position of having no official statements to fall back on when they need to defend their teaching materials and methods. Globalization, free trade, and efforts to impose market models on public services, including education, present dangerous new challenges. The emphasis on individualism and the survival of the richest threatens the central tenets of social responsibility and social justice embedded in equity work. Doing gender-equity work is getting even harder. But as one teacher activist put it, "we are in for the long haul and are not going to be deterred" (J. Wilson, personal communication, 17 April 1996).

Notes

1. In Canada, education is a matter assigned to each of the ten provincial and two territorial governments although the federal government has helped to fund specific school programmes such as technical education or French immersion, provides grants for research in the post-secondary sector and is responsible for the education of aboriginal peoples and the children of military personnel. This paper will focus primarily on one province, Ontario, which is the largest and most populated province though reference will be made to other provinces or regions as well.

2. Ontario has two publicly funded systems, the "public" system and the Roman Catholic separate school system. Both systems follow the provincial curriculum, use Ministry-approved texts, and hire licenced teachers, but in the Roman Catholic system, religious faith is an explicit element in the schools, religious observances and instruction are allowed, and teachers are usually Roman Catholic. Teachers belong to one of five teacher associations. Female public elementary teachers belong to the Federation of Women Teachers Associations of Ontario and male public elementary teachers are members of the Ontario Public School Teachers' Federation. These two federations, after lengthy court disputes about whether compulsory membership clauses based on sex

contravene the Canadian Charter of Rights and Freedoms and the Ontario Human Rights Code, decided in the summer of 1996 to pursue a new union of all public elementary teachers. Teachers in the public secondary schools are members of the Ontario Secondary School Teachers' Federation, and those in the Roman Catholic system belong to the Ontario English Catholic Teachers' Association. Teachers working in francophone schools or programmes within schools are members of the Association des enseignants franco-ontariens. These five teacher organisations work together on matters of common concern under the umbrella of the Ontario Teachers' Federation. The other provinces and territories have one, or at the most two, teacher federations.

3. These conclusions are drawn from my current research-in-progress, which deals with young men and their understandings of gender equality.

References

Acker, S., and K. Oatley. 1993. Gender issues in education for science and technology: Current situation and prospects for change. *Canadian Journal of Education/Revue canadienne de l'éducation* 81(3): 255–72.

Baldwin, P., and D. Baldwin. 1992. The portrayal of women in classroom textbooks. *Canadian Social Studies* 26(3): 110–4.

Barlow, M., and H-J. Robertson. 1994. *Class Warfare: The Assault on Canada's Schools*. Toronto: Key Porter.

Batcher, E., A. Winter, and V. Wright. 1987. *The More Things Change...The More They Stay the Same*. Toronto: Federation of Women Teachers' Associations of Ontario.

Bibby, R. W., and D. C. Posterski,. 1992. *Teen Trends: A Nation in Motion*. Toronto: Stoddart.

Canadian Teachers' Federation. 1990. *Thumbs Down: A Classroom Response to Violence towards Women*. Ottawa: Author.

Coulter, R. P. 1995. Struggling with sexism: Experiences of feminist first-year teachers. *Gender and Education* 7(1): 33–50.

Coulter, R. P. 1996a. Gender equity and schooling: Linking research and policy. *Canadian Journal of Education/Revue canadienne de l'éducation* 21(4): 433–52.

Coulter, R. P. 1996b. School restructuring Ontario style: A gendered agenda. In S. Robertson and H. Smaller, eds., *Teacher Activism in the 1990s*. Toronto: James Lorimer, 89–102.

Coulter, R. P. Forthcoming. "Us guys in suits are back": Women, educational work and the market economy in Canada. In I. Elgqvist-Saltzman, A.

Mackinnon and A. Prentice, eds., *Dangerous Terrain for Women? Education into the Twenty-First Century*. London: Falmer Press.

Eisenstein, H. 1991. *Gender Shock: Practicing Feminism on Two Continents.* Boston: Beacon Press.

Federation of Women Teachers' Associations of Ontario (FWTAO). 1996. *Affirmative Action/Employment Equity*. Toronto: Author.

Gaskell, J., A. McLaren, and M. Novogrodsky. 1989. *Claiming an Education: Feminism and Canadian Schools.* Toronto: Our Schools/Our Selves Education Foundation.

Holmes, J., and E. L. Silverman. 1992. *We're Here, Listen To Us!: A Survey of Young Women in Canada.* Ottawa: Canadian Advisory Council on the Status of Women.

Human Resources Development Canada. 1994. *Profile of Post-Secondary Education in Canada*. 1993 Edition, Ottawa: Minister of Supply and Services Canada.

Julien, L. 1987. *Women's Issues in Education in Canada: A Survey of Policies and Practices at the Elementary and Secondary Levels*. Toronto: Council of Ministers of Education, Canada.

King, A. J. C., and M. J. Peart. 1992. *Teachers in Canada: Their Work and Quality of Life.* Ottawa: Canadian Teachers' Federation.

Larkin, J. 1994. *Sexual Harassment: High School Girls Speak Out.* Toronto: Second Story Press.

Light, B., P. Staton, and P. Bourne. 1989. Sex equity content in history textbooks. *The History and Social Science Teacher* 25(1): 18–20.

MacLeod, L. 1988. *Progress as Paradox: A Profile of Women Teachers*. Ottawa: Canadian Teachers' Federation.

Manitoba Teachers' Society. 1990. *Report of the Task Force on the Physical and Emotional Abuse of Teachers*. Winnipeg: Author.

Maritime Provinces Education Foundation. 1991. *Women's Issues in Education: A Co-operative Approach.* No Place: Author.

Mercer, S. L. 1988. Not a pretty picture: An exploratory study of violence against women in high school dating relationships. *Resources for Feminist Research* 17(2): 15–23.

Naveau, B. 1992. We have a lot to say: Young women for gender equity. *Canadian Woman Studies/Les cahiers de la femme* 12(3): 85–7.

Novogrodsky, M., M. Kaufman, D. Holland, and M. Wells. 1992. Retreat for the future: An anti-sexist workshop for high schoolers. *Our Schools/Our Selves* 3(4): 67–87.

Ontario Ministry of Education. 1975. *The Formative Years. Circular P1J1.* Toronto: Author.

Ontario Ministry of Education. 1988. *Circular 14 Textbooks: Appendix to Circular 14 Evaluation Forms*. Toronto: Author.

Ontario Ministry of Education. 1989. *Ontario Schools: Intermediate and Senior Divisions, Program and Diploma Requirements.* Revised Edition, Toronto: Author.

Ontario Ministry of Education and Training. 1994. *Engendering Equity: Transforming Curriculum (validation draft).* Toronto: Author.

Ontario Secondary School Teachers' Federation, Ontario Women's Directorate, and Ontario Ministry of Education and Training. 1995. *The Joke's Over: Student to Student Sexual Harassment in Secondary Schools.* Toronto: Ontario Secondary School Teachers' Federation.

Ontario Teachers' Federation and Ontario Women's Directorate. 1994. Existing professional development resources: Assessment and recommendations. Unpublished discussion paper.

Popaleni, K. A. 1991. Violence against young women in heterosexual courtship: Teaching girls to resist. *Canadian Woman Studies/ Les cahiers de la femme* 12(1): 84–6.

Robertson, H-J. 1993. *Progress Revisited: The Quality of (Work)Life of Women Teachers.* Ottawa: Canadian Teachers' Federation.

Robertson, S., and Smaller, H. 1996. *Teacher Activism in the 1990s.* Toronto: James Lorimer.

Royal Commission on Learning. 1994. *For the Love of Learning: Report of the Royal Commission on Learning for Ontario.* Toronto: Queen's Printer.

Royal Commission on the Status of Women in Canada. 1970), *Report of the Royal Commission on the Status of Women in Canada.* Ottawa: Information Canada.

Stevenson, J. 1992. *Gender Equity in Ontario Education: Giving Teachers the Tools to Contribute.* Toronto: Ontario Teachers' Federation.

CHAPTER 7

Barriers to Educational Opportunity in Malawi

Karin Hyde

Introduction[1]

In the modern world, educational attainment is an important contributor to socioeconomic status, which in turn has a major impact on the degree to which individuals are able to gain access to the goods and services that affect quality of life.

This is particularly true in developing countries. The likelihood that one can enter the modern sector of the economy, and thus command wages above the poverty line, is increased considerably by schooling. In developing countries, access to education has profound implications not only for quality of life but also for one's very survival; yet in these countries in particular there are enormous barriers to access at even the primary and secondary levels.

Some of the barriers are economic: the results of poverty and low socioeconomic development. For example, countries may be unable to train or retain enough teachers to staff the required number of classrooms; or there might not be the infrastructure, physical or administrative, to support the required number of schools; or certain areas of the country might be less well served than others because of difficult terrain or poor transportation.

Another set of barriers is social. Certain groups of the population may find their access to education or the opportunities offered within the educational system inhibited by characteristics such as, race, ethnicity, religion, region, or gender. Racial or ethnic out-groups might find themselves excluded from certain types of educational institutions. Requirements for entry may vary from region to region or may present obstacles that are more salient for one group than another and result in the under-representation of certain subgroups within the educational system.

However, access is merely the first hurdle. There appear to be barriers to educational opportunity even for those who are lucky enough or persistent enough to gain access to an educational institution. Within both primary and secondary schools, the standard administrative and pedagogical arrangements can lead to a replication of conditions that mirror those in society. The net result is a reduction of access to educational opportunity, through lower performance, and through apparent self-selection into academic areas and streams that have historically offered lower economic returns.

For example, the socioeconomic status of Malawian women in an environment where significant proportions of men are both poor and uneducated is very low. According to the most recent census, only 35.7 percent of women have ever attended school, and of those, 43.5 percent attended for three or fewer years, and therefore are unlikely to have attained permanent literacy. The majority of women, more than 85 percent, are agricultural labourers and although fertility is falling, the average number of births per woman was 5.7 according to the 1987 Census.

Traditionally, women in Malawi have been expected to signal their subordinate status in a number of ways, including kneeling or curtsying when greeting others, and until 1994, there was strictly enforced legislation governing women's dress. Not surprisingly, girls form a minority at secondary and tertiary levels of education.

In this chapter, the secondary schools of Malawi will be used as an example of how educational institutions themselves can restrict educational opportunity for girls, even within a context where the official government policy is to promote the educational participation of girls and women. The discussion will centre on girls in mixed-sex secondary schools and how the social context and the administrative arrangements of the schools combine to produce a situation in which it is difficult for girls to do well academically. At the same time most of the teachers and head-teachers not only have strong expectations that girls will not do well, but, in general, attribute their poor performance to the girls' individual characteristics and not to institutional and pedagogical factors.

This chapter will delineate the major dimensions of girls' education in Malawi, including the contrasts between girls' performance in single- and mixed-sex secondary schools. I will review evidence, based on observation and fieldwork in several secondary boarding schools in early 1993, of the characteristics of the school environment that contribute to poor performance.[1, 2] The final section of this chapter looks at the possibilities for ameliorating the situation. The use of gender streaming in two schools to improve performance is described.

Education in Malawi

Among the countries of the southern region of Africa, Malawi ranks low in the area of female educational participation, particularly with respect to enrolment and performance. At the primary and secondary levels, female enrolment as a proportion of total enrolment was 47 percent and 35 percent respectively in the academic year 1992–3, MOEST (1993). The enrolment levels are in sharp contrast to those found in Botswana, Lesotho, and Swaziland, where girls form a majority at these levels; they also compare unfavourably with other countries in the region, such as Zimbabwe, which had 49.2 percent and 42.3 percent female enrolment at the primary and secondary levels respectively by 1995 (UNESCO 1996).

Primary

Malawi's net enrolment rate for 6–13-year-olds was 55.9 percent in the academic year 1992-1993. The enrolment rate differed by gender, boys having an enrolment rate of 50 percent and girls 54 percent. There is also regional variation in enrolment, ranging from 83.6 percent in the Northern Region, to 52.2 percent in the Central, and 51 percent in the Southern, according to MOEST (1993).

Girls and boys have historically entered standard 1 in very similar numbers. However, females gradually fall away as they move through school. As they enter and pass through puberty, girls experience much pressure to marry and they become more aware of the low probability of proceeding to secondary school because of the low transition rates.

There is a greater propensity for boys to repeat the senior grades in order to increase their chances of entering secondary school; so while 51 percent of standard 1 repeaters were female, only 31 percent of standard 8 repeaters were female in the academic year 1992-1993. This is an indication either that parents are more willing to invest in marginal boys or that boys are more determined and able to repeat.

At the examination that all students take in Standard 8, the primary school leaving examination (PSLE), boys do better in all subjects, including subjects like history and geography that have been shown to be gender neutral in other countries. The smallest difference in performance is in Chichewa, the national language, according to Bradbury (1990).

Secondary

The secondary level admits a much smaller proportion of the relevant cohort. The average transition rate from Standard 8 to Form 1 was approximately 11 percent in 1993 with the transition rate being higher for girls than for boys, although boys have higher scores than girls on the PSLE. As a means of promoting girls' secondary education, the cut-off point for their entry was lowered. As a result, every year for the last ten years for which data is available, the proportion of girls in Form 1 has been higher than the proportion of girls in Standard 8 of the previous year.

Formal secondary education in Malawi comes in two basic forms, in secondary schools and through distance education centres. The centres were begun in an attempt to meet the excess demand for secondary places. They operate as self-study centres, supervised by a teacher-in-charge, who is usually a seconded primary school teacher. Generally, students do not have access to laboratories or other learning materials apart from their workbooks.

Secondary schools in Malawi are of two basic types, day and boarding. In the academic year 1992-1993 there were 118 schools in total, with 45 being private secondary schools. The government day schools enrolled the largest proportion (46 percent), followed by the aided boarding (30.3 percent) and the unaided schools (16.01 percent).

The Junior Certificate examination (JC), taken after two years of secondary education, and the Malawi Certificate of Education examination (MCE), taken after the fourth and final year of secondary education, also present a consistent picture of lower female performance. At the JC examination, the difference in pass rates is usually over 20 percent. In almost all subjects examined for the Malawi Certificate of Education, boys do better than girls. The only subjects in which females do as well as or better than males are Chichewa and Bible Knowledge, according to Kadzamira (1987, 1988). In particular, girls' performance in mathematics and science examinations at the end of secondary schooling is significantly below that of boys (Kadzamira 1987). There is relatively little difference in the proportions passing the examinations by school type.

However, whether a school is single sex or mixed sex does have an impact on the proportion passing the MCE examination, based on data from 1987 to 1991. Girls in co-educational schools had pass rates up to twenty percentage points lower than girls in single-sex schools, while for boys the difference was never higher than eight percentage points. Unfortunately, even girls in single-sex schools have pass rates that are generally 10 percent lower than boys in single-sex schools and approximately 5 percent lower than boys in mixed-sex schools at the MCE level.

Tertiary

At the tertiary level, the proportion of females is still quite low, although it has been rising. In the academic year 1992-1993 it was 22 percent within the university and 31 percent, including the teacher-training colleges. Although the proportion of girls sitting for the MCE from mixed-sex schools has been close to 50 percent since 1989, Hiddleston (1993) indicates that the majority (over 70 percent) of the female entrants to Chancellor College, the Arts and Science faculties of the University of Malawi, have come from single-sex schools since 1986. Although women are predominantly found in traditional subject areas, such as humanities and education, approximately 22 percent of those enrolled are studying science or mathematics (MOEC 1989).

Summary

The two most salient features of female educational participation in Malawi are high dropout rates and low achievement relative to boys. Reasons for this vary; the low socioeconomic status of women, characteristics of the schools themselves, and finally the attitudes and behaviours of parents all have a role to play. I will now focus on the school characteristics that contribute to inhibiting access to educational opportunity for girls.

The School's role

Gender Imbalance

The secondary school in Malawi is primarily a male institution: the majority of the teachers and head teachers are male, male students outnumber female students two to one. There are a number of ways in which this gender imbalance can have a negative effect on the participation of females, both as students and as teachers. For example, Lee, Smith, and Cioci (1993) found in the US that there was an interaction between the gender of the teacher and the gender of the principal that had an impact on teachers' assessments of their own power. Female teachers in schools headed by females saw themselves as more powerful, as having more influence on school policy, being more effective, and having more control over classroom practice, than did female teachers in schools with male principals.

Anecdotal evidence suggests that the presence of female teachers in schools is beneficial to the education of girls (King and Hill 1993). The mechanism through which the presence of female teachers improves girls' participation varies; in some traditional and Muslim societies, the presence of female teachers serves to reassure parents that their daughters will be adequately safeguarded and supervised. Evidence from this study[1] suggests that in secondary schools, there might be an alternative mechanism, that is, through the availability of role models. When students were asked to describe the occupation of the individual they most admired and their own desired occupation, there was a high degree of congruence between the two. The greater presence of female teachers is likely to have an effect if only in widening the occupational choices of the female students. As a minority among students, girls experience a variety of negative effects. There were anecdotal reports from teachers and head-teachers that boys in mixed schools often harass and tease girls who do well. They accuse them of being unfeminine, unnatural, treading on male preserves, and so on. Several teachers attributed the fall-off in performance from Form 1 to Form 4 and the increasing unwillingness of girls to answer questions in class to a reluctance to draw attention to themselves if they were bright, or to invite ridicule if they were not.

A particular instance of harassment arose in a school in which one cohort of girls had been offered the opportunity, on an experimental basis, to take technical drawing, a subject usually reserved for boys, at the start of their school career. The majority dropped the subject after the second year, but three continued and consequently were the only girls in a class of about forty. They were subjected to great pressure from male classmates to drop the subject and move to another class. The head teacher had to intervene to keep the girls in the class.

The idea that some subjects are not appropriate for girls can show up in students' self-ratings of their performance in these subjects. The students were asked to rate themselves in English and mathematics, the two target subjects, and those who considered that their performance was either good or poor were asked to cite explanatory factors. Just over 50 percent of both males and females rated their performance in English as "good". Just under 50 percent of the males felt their performance in mathematics was good, while only 24 percent of the females did so.

Family backgrounds differed quite markedly. The girls' parents were more educated; both were more likely to have some form of post-secondary education, (44.3 percent of girls' fathers against 20.6 percent of boys' and 19.1 percent of girls' mothers against 8.1 percent of boys'). Similarly, there was a very low incidence of "no schooling," 1.5 percent of girls' fathers against 7.3 percent of the boys'. The disparity in family background led to an age difference. Boys were older, 20.9 years on average compared to 19.0 years for girls, and this did not appear to result from a difference in the number of classes repeated: 1.2 versus 1.1. The group of students with the lowest average age were girls whose fathers were in the professional/managerial occupational category and the category with the oldest mean age were boys whose fathers were smallholder farmers. In other words, it appears to be a compositional effect, based on the tendency for more educated parents to send their children to school at an earlier age. This tendency appears to be more pronounced for girls than for boys; girls are younger in every occupational category. Consequently, as a group, the girls are more likely to be vulnerable to intimidation and bullying.

Attitudes towards Female Students

When headteachers were asked to distinguish between the goals of education for male and female students, some clear gender differences emerged. Among headmasters, four of the seven indicated that they did not feel that there was or should be a difference in the goals of education by gender. On the other hand, headmistresses clearly felt that they should offer different things or that girls had particular needs that they should attempt to meet. The female heads stressed a preparation that would allow the girls to obtain some measure of financial independence and one indicated the development of self-worth as a goal. Independence and assertiveness were clear themes for their goals for female students.

Male heads also stressed independence and self-reliance for male students in the context of employment. They indicated that the majority of their students could not expect to find employment and in this environment bemoaned the lack of practical/technical subject offerings and the shortage of teachers in those areas. Female heads also saw self-employment and a general adaptability as important for boys for largely the same reasons.

From this small sample of head teachers, there appears to be a similarity in the way male students are viewed by both male and female heads that is not present with respect to female students. Even those male heads who stressed developing the ability to work with their hands as the major outcome of education, laid much lower emphasis on girls gaining income-generating skills. "Girls can always get married," suggested one. Female heads on the other hand repeatedly referred to social conditions; the high cost of living and the uncertainty of marriage or of one's marriage partner were reasons why they needed to encourage their female students to gain financial independence. Male heads clearly did not feel any personal responsibility in addressing or redressing the social conditions that lead to gender inequities.

Several heads referred spontaneously to the differences in performance between girls in mixed-sex and single-sex schools. Several heads in mixed-sex schools reported on efforts to control the harassment of girls in their schools. At the same time, they noted girls' "laziness," "sense of inferiority," and "lack of ambition" and made reference to cultural beliefs that deemphasise education for females. Again this seemed to be an attempt to distance themselves from any problems that girls might be having in school. The most commonly used strategy for encouraging girls to work hard or avoid pregnancy was counselling or talks by female teachers and seldom by headteachers, especially if these happened to be male.

Teachers' Attitudes towards Students
There was very little difference between male and female teachers with respect to their attitudes towards female students. Most of the female teachers, 77 percent, and 80 percent of the male teachers felt that boys were definitely more interested in schoolwork than girls. Yet a majority of both groups, 60 percent and 65 percent, respectively, felt that girls should not be treated differently. Of the minority that felt that girls should be treated differently, most agreed that discipline, academic standards and subject choice were what should differ.

There was a difference between the sexes regarding teaching methods. Thirty-three percent of the female teachers and 80 percent of the male teachers felt that teaching methods for boys and girls should differ. There seems to be a parallel here to the divergence of opinions of headteachers discussed above. The fact that female teachers indicate that teaching methods should not differ points to a less pro-active stance vis-à-vis education of girls than among male teachers. Presumably a belief that teaching methods should differ reflects a greater willingness on the part of male teachers to modify their teaching to accommodate girls. The fact that they are younger and better educated than female teachers probably contributes to this willingness.

The teachers' responses to a series of questions about the characteristics of boys and girls showed a great deal of congruence between the sexes. However, when teachers are separated by the type of school in which they teach, some differences do emerge.

Female teachers in single-sex schools are least likely to agree with any of the five statements meant to describe generally-held beliefs about girls in school, except that girls receive more parental support than do boys. Female teachers in mixed-sex schools were most likely to agree that girls are shyer and that boys performed better. However, they were also most likely to agree that girls should have the same education as boys. The male teachers showed smaller differences based on the type of school in which they taught than did the female teachers.

Finally, both female and male teachers were equally split as to whether boys and girls had different learning styles. Those who felt they did generally indicated that girls were more passive. They referred to more questioning from boys, more time spent studying, and more time spent note-taking in class as indications of boys' more active approach to learning.

Reported Attitudes of Male Teachers

An attempt was made to get each teacher to indicate whether s/he felt that male teachers differed from female teachers in their attitudes towards female students. A majority of both sexes felt that male teachers did not differ from female teachers. A number of male teachers indicated that on the contrary it was female teachers who were most likely to treat female students negatively, because "they envied them their youth." Some female teachers felt that male teachers were too lenient, and let female students get away with too much. Thus the impression was created that their standards of performance and behaviour need not be as high as boys' and this undermined their opportunities in school.

Female teachers in single-sex schools were most likely to declare that there was no difference between male and female teachers, and female teachers in mixed-sex schools were least likely to feel there was no difference. There was no difference between male teachers in single-sex and mixed-sex schools.

Attitudes of Teachers in General

Teachers were asked to characterize general teacher attitudes to male and female students, as distinct from their own personal attitudes, on ten dimensions.

Only a minority of male and female teachers in both types of schools felt that teachers in general thought that boys and girls did not differ on the dimensions presented to them. Among male teachers in mixed-sex schools, the category "educational barriers facing boys and girls" was the dimension which the smallest number felt was the same for both sexes; "interest in schoolwork" was the dimension where the largest percentage saw no difference. Among females in mixed-sex schools, there was a general perception that as far as the administrative dimensions of school were concerned, for example, attendance and punctuality, boys and girls did not differ; however, class participation and academic preferences were seen as the sources of greatest differences.

In single-sex schools, male teachers saw very little similarity between male and female students. With respect to the general subject of interest in education, that is, interest in school work, value of education, and academic preferences, no male teacher in a single-sex school felt that boys and girls were similar. No more than 30 percent saw similarity in any of the other dimensions. Female teachers in single-sex schools were more like their colleagues, both male and female, in mixed-sex schools than like the male teachers in single-sex schools. Although they also felt that academic preferences of boys and girls were not at all similar, 87.5 percent of them felt that boys and girls had a similar degree of interest in schoolwork. It is noteworthy however that only 12.5 percent of female teachers in single-sex schools felt that female students had the same ability as male students.

Teachers in single-sex schools, both male and female, appeared to be happier with parents' level of concern for their children. Eighty-seven percent of the females and 90 percent of the males rated their level of concern as "good" or "adequate". Approximately 65 percent of teachers in mixed-sex schools held the same view.

Male teachers in single-sex schools (90 percent) and female teachers in mixed-sex schools (83.3 percent) were most likely to feel that the school encouraged the education of girls.

Little difference was observed in the questioning behaviour of teachers, except that male mathematics teachers were least likely to direct questions to girls. It was also more common to find group work as a supplement to whole-class instruction in single-sex schools.

Curricular and Administrative Policies

Pregnancy
The current policy for all levels of education is that girls who become pregnant must leave school. Since 1993, they can be re-admitted at all

levels, if they can prove that adequate arrangements have been made for the care of the child. To carry out this policy, each educational institution is supposed to arrange for the medical examination of all female students once each term, or three times a year. Girls found to be pregnant are asked to leave immediately; the regulation requires that if a boy within the educational system is to blame, he must also leave. The boy is allowed to re-enrol if he promises to marry the girl. Previously, the girl was not supposed to re-enrol on the grounds that she is likely to corrupt other students, and there is still a great reluctance on the part of head teachers to re-admit girls to the same institution. There are no sanctions for males outside the educational system. Sagawa and Thawe (1992) estimate that 76 percent of girls who drop out from secondary school do so because they become pregnant.

Whilst the revised policy has provided an opportunity for pregnant girls who wish to continue their education, it is not an opportunity of which many can take advantage. Unless she has parents able and willing to support the child, or gets the father to support the child, the responsibility is hers and this responsibility can seldom be combined with formal study. The likelihood that girls will become pregnant and leave school before they complete the cycle is an important reason why parents regard investment in their daughters' education as more risky than that of their sons'.

In secondary school, there is a standard set of subject options, some of which are determined by sex. Until recently, it was government policy that girls must take home economics and needlework and boys take woodwork/technical drawing. This is no longer government policy, but few schools offer open choice. Institutional inertia, headteachers' convictions that all girls must take home economics, and teacher resistance to teaching mixed-sex or cross-sex classes for these subjects that were formerly meant for one sex or the other, all contribute to the slow pace of change. In some schools, however, subjects such as French or history are scheduled at the same time as home economics, which effectively shuts out females from those subjects.

Traditionally, in Malawi children are supposed to kneel when speaking to their parents. This practice is carried over to secondary school because teachers are regarded as *in loco parentis*, but with the difference that it is only strictly enforced for girls. Male students were seldom observed kneeling when they spoke to teachers and even those who did were more likely to crouch than actually kneel.

Finally, for a variety of reasons, the movement of girls around the school compound is more strictly regulated than that of boys. Girls were usually expected to be in their dorms after dark and in bed with lights out by 9 or 10 p.m. Boys, on the other hand, were free to use classrooms and other rooms for study after school hours and needed only to report to the dorm in time for lights out. Similarly, in the morning, boys could come and study in the classrooms in the early morning before school, while girls are again confined to their dormitories. This is clearly in order to safeguard girls' physical and sexual safety, but the net result is to reduce considerably the opportunities for study, particularly in mixed-sex schools, as dormitories are usually overcrowded.

The ultimate consequence of these and other school policies is to limit the educational opportunities for girls during their school career, by making them vulnerable to involuntary withdrawals, by limiting the subjects they can study, by reducing the time available for study, and by impressing a subservient status, even vis-à-vis fellow male students.

Compensatory Measures

The picture painted above is bleak. However, it should be stressed that there is a lot of concern at various levels of the education system about the position of girls. The government of Malawi has made great efforts to promote female education and, with donor assistance, has instituted a number of measures that stress increasing access and decreasing dropout in school.

These measures include the setting of quotas for entrance into secondary and tertiary levels of education, the provision of scholarships for girls who wish to study "non-traditional" subjects at tertiary level, the removal of restrictions on the subjects females can study at the secondary and tertiary level, and the recently announced scholarships for all secondary school girls.

A major programme known as GABLE, jointly sponsored by the Government of Malawi and the United States Agency for International Development has used a multifaceted approach since 1990 to promote basic education for girls. This has involved the building of schools and teachers' houses, input into the revision of the curriculum, rebates of school fees for non-repeating girls[3]. The most recent innovation is a social-mobilization campaign aimed at persuading parents to send their daughters to school and keep them there.

These measures have shown some success in improving access, but there is little evidence that they are having any effect on girls' performance.

Individual secondary school teachers carry out experiments to increase the performance of girls: 50 percent of the female teachers in single-sex schools claimed to have done so. These ranged from more intensive teaching in the classroom, encouragement of group work, extra instruction outside the class, and more questioning of girls.

At the school level, a number of schools had introduced various measures to improve girls' performance. Three main strategies were being used. The first involved tighter control of female students' use of designated study time, the second involved some form of separation of the sexes during instruction and the third relied on talks and counselling by female teachers.

The staff at one school had associated girls' poor performance on the JC and MCE examinations with their poor attendance at prep. Consequently, attendance at prep had been made compulsory at the beginning of the year and anyone with more than five absences was asked to leave the boarding department; this had already happened to one girl. The attendance at prep had improved but it was still too early to judge the effect on performance.

Another school had initiated separate prep sessions; all the girls had to study in the hall under supervision while boys were free to study where they chose. Among girls' schools, dormitories were usually locked during class time, so girls could not use them for naps or skipping classes, a problem in some mixed-sex schools that did not lock their dormitories during school hours.

Two schools had started, but later abandoned, gender streaming, abandoned apparently on the grounds that it violated the principal benefit of mixed-sex schooling: the opportunity for the sexes to interact during the adolescent years.

One of the questions asked of both teachers and head teachers during the project fieldwork was whether they had conducted experiments or made any changes in the way they taught specifically in order to improve the performance of girls. Three schools and about fifteen teachers said they had done so, and in four cases achievement data was obtained from the teacher or school to document the impact of the experiment.

The two cases (schools) for which data of adequate quality were obtained are discussed below. The other two situations did not have enough data for any conclusions to be drawn. In one case, the teacher had kept incomplete records. In the other, the school only provided scores for the first year of the experiment of gender streaming, in which the girls had been in mixed classes for two terms and separated for the last. The two experiments reported on here involved forms of gender streaming.

In common with virtually all mixed-sex schools in Malawi, the populations in both schools were about 30 percent female. School A had initiated its experiment, which ended in 1994, with the 1980 entering cohort. The experiment in School B was initiated in 1990 and continued for two years, before it was discontinued on the grounds that the principal advantage of mixed-sex schooling was being abrogated.

School A

The experiment began with the 1980 intake, which was examined at JC in 1982 and MCE in 1984. By chance, the mathematics teachers in this school have all been, for several years, expatriate females. Very early on they became aware of the significant differences between male and female performance in mathematics at the JC and MCE levels. They also noticed the negative attitudes girls had towards the subject and the fact that girls who did like mathematics were disparaged by male classmates. The teachers, with the co-operation of the headmaster and the Ministry of Education, decided to employ two-way streaming in mathematics, by gender and by ability. There were three mixed-ability streams in Form 1 and these were reorganized for the purposes of mathematics instruction into four groups as follows:

1. Top 32 boys
2. Bottom 25 boys
3. Top 32 girls
4. Bottom 25 girls

These groups were placed in separate classes. For the 1992 MCE, the classes were divided as follows: top 36 boys in one class, top 36 girls in one class, and the rest of the boys and girls in a third class.

The number of students has been increasing in recent years, making class sizes larger. During the past five years there has been no staff turnover. Three teachers have taught all year groups for the past five years and the same teacher has taught the JC course for two years; the same teacher has taught the MCE course for two years.

Female pass rates at JC went from just over 20 percent in 1981 (before the innovation) to over 80 percent between 1988 and 1991. A decline to 70 percent in 1992 was attributed to an unusually poor performing intake in 1990. Boys also benefitted; their pass rates moved from approximately 70 percent to close to 100 percent in 1988.

The MCE results also show a consistent upward trend to approximately 60 percent and 80 percent from approximately 20 percent and 40 percent in 1982. The school's overall pass rates for the MCE, which were obtained from the Malawi National Examinations Board, do not show a parallel improvement, and therefore, it is clear that the mathematics results are not simply part of an overall change or improvement in the school's results.

The streaming has done two things, raised performance of *both* boys and girls at JC and MCE and narrowed the differential between them at JC level at a cost that is essentially zero.

School B

Again in School B, the teaching staff had noted the gender differentials in performance in all subjects. Here, teachers decided that they would replicate the conditions prevailing in a single-sex secondary school by reserving one of the three streams for girls. Therefore, girls and boys were completely separated for all instruction and only interacted outside class time. The experiment continued for two years, so that in 1990 the entering girls were separated and kept apart for two years. However, the class that entered the next year was not separated.

The evidence from this school consists of end-of-term marks for up to three and a half years for the cohort that was separated as well as the cohort that preceded it and was taught in mixed classes.

The girls who had spent the first two years in a separate class had a higher mean score for every subject except home economics, which is usually taught in sex-segregated classes irrespective of what is happening in the other classes. The means of the two groups were tested in every subject using a t-test. The hypothesis that the means were significantly different was supported at the 5-percent level for every subject except mathematics and agriculture and at the 1-percent level for most of the other subjects.

The evidence from School B appears to support the hypothesis that if girls are put in a separate learning environment, even within a mixed school, it is possible to raise their level of performance. The possibility that the first cohort was more able than the second cannot be dismissed. However, the fact that the two cohorts had been admitted into the same school would suggest that their levels of ability would be generally comparable.

The explanations volunteered for these effects by the teachers themselves mainly centred around the absence of boys in the class. By themselves, girls were said to be more competitive. Removing the intimidation of boys released girls' inhibitions about performing well and therefore led to improved achievement. These explanations do not, however, explain the improved performance of the boys, unless one sees the girls as being a distraction when they are in class with boys.

The experimental nature of the innovation could have led both teachers and students to have raised expectations, thereby improving performance, the so-called Hawthorne effect. However, the sustained improvement in School A casts some doubt on that explanation. A more systematic enquiry into the apparent success of this strategy is clearly required.

Conclusion

To sum up, in mixed schools, there is a situation in which females form a minority, approximately 30 percent in virtually all schools; they are younger; and females are reported to be subjected to verbal and psychological harassment when they show signs of high performance. Finally, the evidence from the gender-streaming experiments in both schools indicates that when they are separated for instruction, a marked improvement in achievement can occur for both genders. Despite the structural bias within schools against women and an unfavourable labour market, it is possible to make institutional changes within the school that will undermine rather than reinforce the disadvantages that women face in society.

Notes

1. Twelve schools, eight mixed and four single-sex, were randomly selected from the list of boarding schools that admitted girls. Within each school, the head teacher, all teachers of mathematics and English in Forms 3 and Form 4, and a systematic random sample of between thirty-five and forty students were selected for interview. In addition, two classroom observations were conducted for each teacher interviewed and a survey of school facilities and conditions conducted.

2. The research on which this paper is based was conducted when the author was a research fellow at the Centre for Social Research, University of Malawi. The funding was provided by The Rockefeller Foundation under their "Re-Entry Support for African Scholars Program."

3. Fees were abolished for all pupils in the academic year 1994–1995 and this has eroded the relative advantage of girls.

References

Bradbury, R. 1990. *Differences between the Results of Boys and Girls in the Subjects of the Primary School Leaving Examinations.* Zomba: Malawi National Examinations Board.

Government of Malawi. 1993. *Malawi Population and Housing Census 1987, Vol. 1 & 2.* Zomba: National Statistical Office.

Hiddleston, P. 1993. The achievement of women in mathematics and science subjects: A case study at the University of Malawi. *Southern African Journal of Mathematics and Science Education.* 1: 49–57.

Hyde, K.A.L. 1993. *Instructional and Institutional Barriers to Girls' Achievement in Secondary Schools in Malawi: Preliminary Survey Results.* Zomba: Centre for Social Research, University of Malawi.

Kadzamira, E.C. 1987. *Sex Differences in the Performance of Candidates in MSCE Mathematics and Science Subjects, 1982–1986.* Zomba: Malawi National Examinations Board.

Kadzamira, E.C. 1988. *Sex Differences in Performance of Candidates in Languages and Humanities Subjects at MSCE Level, 1982–1986.* Zomba: Malawi National Examinations Board.

King, E.M., and M.A. Hill, eds. 1993. *Women's Education in Developing Countries: Barriers, Benefits and Policies.* Baltimore and London: John Hopkins University Press,

Lee, V.E, J.B. Smith, and M. Cioci. 1993. Teachers and principals: gender-related perceptions of leadership and power in secondary schools. *Educational Evaluation and Policy Analysis* 15(2): 153–80.

Ministry of Education and Culture (MOEC), Planning Division. 1991. *Education Indicators for Malawi, 1985-1989.* Lilongwe: Government of Malawi.

Ministry of Education, Science and Technology (MOEST), Planning Division. 1993. *Basic Education Statistics.* Lilongwe: Government of Malawi.

Sagawa, J., and L. Thawe. 1991. *Wastage of Girls in Secondary Schools in Malawi.* Report produced for USAID. Lilongwe: Government of Malawi.

UNESCO/African Academy of Sciences. 1996. *Female Participation in Education in Sub-Saharan Africa: Statistical Profiles.* Nairobi: Academy Science Publishers.

World Bank. (1990. *Zimbabwe: A Review of Primary and Secondary Education from Successful Expansion to Equity of Learning Achievements.* Washington, D.C.: World Bank.

CHAPTER 8

Education and Gender Equality in Asia

Swarna Jayaweera

The role of education has been analysed from theoretical stances that reflect its multifaceted contributions to "human capital" for economic growth or human resources development, socioeconomic mobility for individuals, social transformation through reduction in inequalities and changing values, and social stratification through the reproduction of social relations and the transfer of "cultural capital" (Schultz 1963; Bourdieu and Passeron 1977; Halsey, Heath and Ridge 1980). In these accounts, gender equality has not been an explicit concern in any theory but is, in fact, a cross-cutting issue manifested through the gender division of labour, gender stratification through degree of access to assets and resources, and underlying gender ideologies and related social norms. This chapter will examine trends in education policies and their outcomes for women in the context of gender equality or inequality in access to education, in the labour market, in decision making in public life, and in the family, drawing from the experiences of ten countries in East, Southeast, and South Asia.

Asia has a rich diversity of cultures and different social and economic systems that have evolved from the interface of traditional cultures and social, economic, and political institutions translocated by imperial powers. The colonial experience under Portuguese, Spanish, Dutch, British, French, American or Japanese colonial administrations varied in duration and intensity in these countries, but left their mark on modernizing institutions such as education systems and on value orientation. In more recent years of increasing interdependence, the international environment, global economic developments and macroeconomic forces have had their impact on industrializing countries, on countries in transition to market economies, and on agrarian societies in the region. Women have been exposed to all these forces and have been affected positively also by international norms pertaining to educational opportunity and women's rights.

Education policies and gender equality in educational opportunity

Modern education systems with an elitist ethos in post-primary education were established in most countries during the colonial period in the nineteenth century. Policies to develop national education systems were introduced in the post-colonial era around the middle of the twentieth century, with the exception of Japan, which started its modernization process in 1868 with the restoration of Emperor Meiji after two centuries of rule by feudal lords. Policymakers in all countries attached importance to extending educational opportunities as an instrument of social and economic advancement. National constitutions enunciated the goal of compulsory education, chiefly at primary or elementary level, but the statement and restatement of this goal in national development plans was in many countries a rhetorical exercise until the UN Convention on the Rights of the Child (1989) and the UN World Conference on Education at Jomtien, Thailand, (1990) created a momentum for plans of action for compulsory primary education, and "education for all," with particular emphasis on the underprivileged.

Two broad strands of education policies can be discerned in the region. Some countries have depended on macrosocial and education policies complemented by supportive facilities and services without gender differentiation, to extend educational opportunities to as many participants as possible. Others have sought to introduce special policies and programmes focussed on girls and women in educationally disadvantaged communities and locations. The macrostatistical data in table 1 points to a congruence between these policy stances and outcomes pertaining to access to and retention in education, while microstudies have documented the influence of several intervening variables in determining these outcomes.

Around fifteen countries in Asia appear to have implemented broad but purposeful national policies in extending educational opportunities. Compulsory education regulations have been in operation in countries such as Japan, Korea, Singapore, China, and the Philippines and are being introduced in Indonesia and Sri Lanka. However, only three countries, Japan, the Republic of Korea, and Singapore have achieved universal primary education and near-universal secondary education.

The provision of educational facilities has been seen as a national priority. Japan expanded education facilities after the 1947 reforms, and

Korea and Singapore concomitantly with their "economic miracles" since the 1960s (Matsui 1996). Malaysia not only used its economic resources to provide facilities, but offered universal, free, primary and secondary education, as well as incentives in the form of scholarships, bursaries and hostel accommodation for students from the rural sector, and introduced affirmative policies to increase the enrolment of Malays who had been educationally disadvantaged (Sidin 1996). Indonesia used new resources generated by the oil boom to improve the physical and social infrastructure, including the introduction of extensive primary education facilities in the 1970s and the expansion of lower secondary education facilities since 1983, leaving upper secondary education as yet largely to private enterprises (Oey-Gardiner and Riga-Adiwoso 1996).

On the other hand, countries such as China in East Asia, the Philippines in Southeast Asia, and Sri Lanka in South Asia, implemented positive macroeducation policies despite resource constraints. China has concentrated on primary and lower secondary education since the 1949 revolution, and stipends offered to low-income families obviated the need for parents to choose between the educational needs of sons and daughters (Mak 1996). In the Philippines, extensive educational provision, free elementary education, and the perception of parents that education provided an avenue of escape from poverty, accelerated the utilization of educational opportunities (Ilo 1990). In Sri Lanka, despite the absence of compulsory education regulations, educational opportunity has been extended due to a strong commitment on the part of the state from the 1940s to reducing socioeconomic inequalities through the provision of educational opportunities; the implementation of free primary, secondary and tertiary (including university) education from 1945; incentives such as island-wide scholarships at Grade 5 and university entrance, free textbooks, uniforms, mid-day meals, and subsidized transport to schools; the provision of a network of primary schools and rural secondary schools; as well as parental perceptions of education as an agent of upward socioeconomic mobility (Jayaweera 1995a, 1996).

In all these countries, macroeducation policies have not reflected specific gender concerns. They have relied on undifferentiated policies to universalize education, while outcomes of macroeducational policies have been accelerated by parental perceptions of the instrumental value of education as an agent of advancement of their sons and daughters and their families. Consequently, female gross enrolment rates at primary level are over 80 percent and overall female literacy rates are over 70 percent, with much higher literacy rates among younger groups of women. However, in around half the secondary school-age population, both girls and boys are being denied educational opportunity in low-

Table 1. Female Educational Participation – Asia (%)

Country	Female Literacy Rate	Male Literacy Rate	Female Gross Enrolment Rates			Female percentage of Total Enrolment		
			Primary school age 6-11 yrs.	Secondary school age 12-17 yrs.	Tertiary Education 18-23 yrs.	Primary school age 6-11 yrs.	Secondary school age 12-17 yrs.	Tertiary Education 18-23 yrs.
Japan	99	99	100	98.2	19.5	49	49	38
Hongkong	86	NA	100	85.3	19.4	48	51	35
Republic of Korea	95	99	100	81.8	24.0	49	47	30
Singapore	84	92	100	87.8	19.9	47	50	42
Brunei	81	NA	80.3	82.2	27.9	98	52	51
Thailand	92	96	81.4	34.6	16.2	49	49	46
Malaysia	72	89	93.1	66.7	7.0	49	51	47
Sri Lanka	85	94	100	64.3	12.3	48	51	42
Philippines	90	90	82.6	76.3	27.6	49	50	63
Indonesia	77	91	92.6	57.7	13.8	48	45	36
Mongolia	75	NA	64.1	89.8	25.8	50	52	58
China	68	92	80.7	36.3	12.3	46	42	33
Maldives	93	93	100	84.2	—	49	49	28
Vietnam	84	93	91.4	44.9	1.9	48	47	28
Myanmar	72	90	92.9	23.9	6.4	48	47	50
Papua New Guinea	48	82	55.3	17.4	2.0	NA	NA	NA
Lao PDR	41	NA	64.0	35.4	4.2	43	42	37
India	35	64	67.8	32.6	6.2	41	36	33
Bangladesh	33	49	58.0	13.3	1.7	45	31	17
Pakistan	22	49	20.6	10.1	2.2	34	29	28
Nepal	14	39	43.9	21.1	2.4	32	27	20
Cambodia	24	52	16	NA	NA	45	30	20
Bhutan	26	55	16.2	6.3	0.4	37	24	17
Afghanistan	15	48	14.1	10.2	1.9	33	33	14

Source: UNDP Human Development Report 1994, 1995
UNESCO Statistical Annual Year Book 1990 (Female percentage of total enrolment)

income countries with resource constraints and relative poverty, such as Sri Lanka and China, and in countries such as Malaysia and Indonesia, where rapid educational expansion has been a recent phenomenon. At the same time, gender disparities are minimal or non-existent at primary and secondary level (table 1). In fact, there have been more girls than boys in secondary schools in countries such as Japan, the Philippines, Sri Lanka and Malaysia, for around two decades. It appears from microstudies that non-schooling in these countries is not pervasive and is concentrated in pockets of poverty in low-income urban neighbourhoods, in deprived or remote villages and, in Sri Lanka and Malaysia, in plantations. It could be surmised that social class rather than gender affected the utilization of educational opportunities in these countries.

Few of this group of countries have more than 20 percent of the relevant age group in tertiary education institutions. Participation rates in the majority of these countries range between 5 percent and 10 percent as the policy focus has been chiefly on primary and secondary education, and resource constraints have limited expansion of facilities in the public sector in many countries. More than 60 percent of tertiary-level students are women in the Philippines and except in East Asia, the percentage of women students is between 40 and 50 percent. It appears to be a manifestation of gender inequality that only around one-third of tertiary-level students are women in economically advanced countries such as Japan and the Republic of Korea, and in China, despite its strong political drive towards equality.

It is also significant that unlike in other countries, there is clearly "gender streaming" in higher education institutions in Japan, the most industrialized country in Asia, since 80 percent of two-year junior college students and only 22 percent of four-year university students were women in 1991. Women aspirants to higher education are said to prefer the less competitive and more "feminine" junior colleges, and parents are said to prefer a university education for their sons and junior colleges for their daughters (Matsui 1996). It is likely that national policies that promote differentiation in opportunities within the higher education system reinforce gender inequality in access to resources such as knowledge and skills at the apex of the education system.

Gender issues as a policy concern surfaced in these countries as a consequence of International Women's Year (1975), the UN Decade for Women (1976–1985), UN World Conferences on Women from Mexico (1975) to Beijing (1995), and the establishment of national mechanisms for women's affairs. These concerns led to developments such as, for instance, the Philippine Development Plan for Women (1989–1992), the Philippine Plan for Gender Responsive Development (1995–2025); and the Children's Charter (1991), Women's Charter (1993), and the National Plan of Action for Women (1996) in Sri Lanka. In the context of the relative gender equality in educational opportunity already achieved in these countries, the implications of these proposals for education policy and practice were largely in the areas of socialization and skills development.

The second strand in national policies that attempted to focus on interventions to meet the 'special" needs of girls and women is characteristic for instance, of India, Bangladesh and Pakistan, which at the time of political independence from British colonial rule in 1947 formed the Indian subcontinent in South Asia, and their northern neighbour, Nepal, which emerged as a modern state in the 1950s.

These countries had the same goals of universalizing at least primary education as the earlier group of countries. The Indian Constitution of 1947 envisaged the goal of compulsory education from six to fourteen years and equal educational opportunity within ten years. In the same year the Pakistan Education Conference advocated five years of free and compulsory education. On its independence from Pakistan in 1971, Bangladesh favoured eight years of compulsory free education. These aspirations were largely confined to constitutions and five-year development plans until recent years. Nepal introduced three years of free primary education in 1971, in India some states introduced compulsory primary education in the 1980s, and the fourth five-year development plan in Bangladesh introduced compulsory education from six to ten years from 1992. In the 1990s national policies for "Education for All" were formulated in these countries after the Jomtien World Conference.

In addition, all these countries specified targets for the enrolment of boys and girls in their five-year development plans — targets which were invariably never met and were reiterated or extended in each successive plan. Specific strategies were also proposed to increase the enrolment of girls. These strategies became more important with the declaration of 1990 as SAARC's (South Asian Association for Regional Co-operation) "Year of the Girl Child" and 1991–2000 as the SAARC's "Decade of the Girl Child."

In Bangladesh, following the introduction of free primary education, the fourth five-year plan (1991–1995) proposed free education for girls to Grade 8. Scholarships, free books, and free uniforms have been provided for girls in poverty groups and remote areas and more women teachers were recruited. A "Food for Education" programme has been introduced in low-income neighbourhoods. A mass literary campaign was started in the 1980s, but failed to achieve its objectives (Islam 1982; Khan 1992).

In India, despite governmental five-year plans, the education of girls received inadequate attention until the Report of the Committee on the Status of Women (1974) stimulated action. Reliance was placed chiefly on nonformal education centres to increase the literacy levels of girls and women and to extend education opportunities to girls out of school in the 6–14 age group. The National Policy on Education (1986) took a more holistic view, giving priority to the education of women for equality, to the use of education as an agent of change in the status of women and to play a "positive interventionist role" in the empowerment of women (MHRD, 1986). The Plan of Action (1992) spelled out measures, including plans with a specific focus on girls and women to universalize primary education and adult education. The National Literacy Mission (1988), modified as a Total Literacy Campaign in selected districts, has a strong conscientization component for illiterate women which has been found to have empowered groups of women.

Nepal had a late start with the establishment of its modern school for girls in Kathmandu in 1952. Special programmes have focussed on girls in remote areas and in low-income families from the 1970s. In addition to the free distribution of textbooks nationwide in grades 1–3 in the primary school, books were distributed free among girls in grades 4 and 5 in remote districts. Scholarships and free uniforms were given to girls from low-income families to enable them to attend school, and annual prizes were awarded to schools that enrolled the most girls. Nepal also had a special programme from the early 1970s, supported by UNESCO and subsequently by UNICEF, to train young women in remote areas as teachers so that they would return to their districts and enrol more girls in schools. Hostels were attached to schools in educationally disadvantaged districts to provide girls with secondary education before they entered the teacher training programme. Literacy classes were conducted for girls outside of school in remote areas. The seventh five-year plan (1985–1990) proposed free primary and secondary education for girls. Pakistan's five-year plans recognized the gender gap and proposed to increase the number of girls' schools, but even the Mohalla schools (classes held in the residences of women teachers to encourage parents to enrol their daughters) were very limited in number. The new education programme (1992–2000) also does not reflect gender-specific priorities.

Despite efforts to improve the participation of girls in education, data presented in table 1 indicates that female literacy rates range between 14 and 35 percent, and gross female primary enrolment rates between 20 and 68 percent in these countries. It appears unlikely too that universal primary education and gender equality even at the first level of education will be achieved in the year 2000 as envisaged in national plans. Gross female secondary and tertiary education enrolment rates are very low, at less than 35 and 7 percent, respectively. Gender disparities are very wide and have even widened in the 1980s in Pakistan and Nepal. Both India and Pakistan have invested more heavily in secondary and higher education than in primary education, but the benefits from this investment as well as from developments in Bangladesh and Nepal have accrued largely to the middle classes. The elitist or middle-class ethos of secondary and tertiary education institutions in these countries has been a focus of criticism (Chanana 1988; Huq 1992).

Problems faced in moving rapidly towards gender equality in these countries are rooted in economic, political and social structural constraints. As low-income countries, they lack the economic resources of many of the countries in East Asia and Southeast Asia to provide adequate education facilities. But they also appear to have had less commitment at policy level than countries with resource constraints such as China, the Philippines and Sri Lanka. Critics in these four countries have commented on the largely welfare approach to education, particularly in the early decades, poor resource allocation even within budgetary constraints, unrealistic targets, little action and weak implementation of programmes (Khan 1992; Jabbar 1992; Acharya 1994; Chowdhury 1996). It is possible also that the incentives offered to parents to send their daughters to schools were inadequate to counter their prejudices or their poverty status as they were often limited to primary education, which was not expected to ensure substantial economic rewards. From a gender perspective, their difficulties were compounded by the fact that their societies were less liberal or egalitarian than, for instance, the Philippines and Sri Lanka.

In these four countries, the majority of parents saw little value in education for their daughters, who were expected to marry very early and be confined to their homes as wives and mothers. Strong "son preference" based on cultural assumptions of men as providers for families determined priority in the allocation of resources within families for the education of sons. In the joint family structure, girls would be "lost" to the natal family on marriage, and investment in their education was perceived to be a waste of scarce resources. In low-income families, girls were an economic asset from the early age of six or seven in their assigned tasks of household chores, including collecting water, fuel and firewood, child-care tasks, care of animals and farming. A young girl in Nepal is estimated to work almost as many hours as an adult male and cannot therefore enrol in schools. This low demand for education is further exacerbated by constraints in the supply factor: distance to school, difficult terrain and the lack of girls' schools and women teachers in the face of opposition to co-education in Pakistan and in some communities in the other countries (Chanana 1988; Huq 1992; Acharya 1994). The disadvantaged situation of the girl child in these countries is underscored even in the Platform for Action adopted at the World Conference in Beijing in 1995.

It is important to note that gender equality in education cannot be achieved by access to and retention in the education system alone. Gender equality in the external environment depends also on the personality development of girls and women and the equitable distribution of knowledge and skills. If education is to be an effective agent of equality, it has to ensure that the products of the education system are equally equipped to control the direction of their lives and to use the knowledge and skills they have acquired to further their advancement in the adult world.

Education as an agent of socialisation has tended to reinforce stereotypes that create or reproduce gender inequalities in all countries, irrespective of literacy and enrolment rates. Educational materials reflect gender-role stereotypes that portray girls and women in subordinate positions and in conventional nurturing and servicing roles (Bisaria 1985; Jarillas and Diaz 1994). Schools condition differential behavioural norms for girls and boys, expecting girls to be obedient, passive and quiet, and boys to be assertive and independent (KWDI 1985 and 1986; NCRFW 1995). Girls in countries such as Sri Lanka and the Philippines tend to be exposed to a dual agenda, to aspire to the highest educational and employment levels but to be subservient in behaviour (Jayaweera 1993). Consequently, many girls tend to develop negative self-perceptions, to lack self-confidence and to limit their aspirations and future options (Hassan 1982). They are apt to enter the world of work or marriage with less initiative and confidence than do men.

Access to higher education does not appear to contribute to reducing such impediments to equality. It has been claimed that higher education does not raise consciousness and empower women to be agents of change in their own lives and as catalysts of social transformation (Mazumdar 1989; Huq 1992; Shamim 1995). Surveys have found that a significant proportion of female university students admit that they lack self-confidence (UNESCO 1990). University graduates do not always challenge social practices such as dowry bargaining and virginity tests that negate their personhood. Dowry deaths and female foeticide and infanticide have been reported in "educated families" in India.

Only two countries have proposed national policies to counter the impact of negative socialization by curriculum and textbook revision and other supportive measures. In India, the National Centre for Education, Research and Training (NCERT) has a special department that has prepared gender-fair curriculum materials. The Plan of Action (1992), of the National Policy for Education (MHRD 1986) proposes promoting a positive image of women through the common core curriculum and developing guidelines for the preparation of materials that will promote gender equality. The Philippine Development Plan for Women (1989–1992) drawn up by the National Committee on the Role of Filipino Women (NCRFW), promoted programmes to eliminate sexism in the curriculum and educational materials, and to introduce career-orientation and gender-sensitization programmes, The Philippine Plan for Gender Responsive Development (1995–2025), noted that access to education was no longer a problem but proposed the formulation of a set of criteria to eliminate gender bias in curricula and textbooks and the development of gender-fair messages to be incorporated into curriculum content. It is perhaps premature to assess the impact of policies in the two countries to promote more equitable gender relations in the economy, society and family.

The only intervention at the level of higher education has been the organization of women's studies programmes in universities, women's colleges, and research institutions, following developments in western universities. Around 20 to 25 percent of universities and colleges in Japan had introduced such courses by the end of the 1980s, and these are said to have increased consciousness of gender issues (Matsui 1996). The Philippine Plans for Gender Responsive Development (1995–2025) proposed the organization of a Women's Studies Consortium that included seven major higher-education institutions. In India, the University Grants Commission established a link scheme of twenty-two women's studies centres and eleven cells in universities and colleges. Indiresan (1995), in a review of these centres in 1993, found them to be weak in resources, infrastructure, and quality of work, and to be compartmentalized in the higher education structure. In other countries, women's studies programmes in educational institutions have been few in number, low in visibility, and are hardly likely to empower a significant number of women.

Another determinant of the relationship between education and gender equality is the distribution of vocationally related knowledge and skills, a corollary of the socialization process in educational institutions. In most countries, regardless of participation rates, girls in secondary schools are directed to home economics and boys to technical courses within the general education system or in vocational secondary schools, irrespective of their aptitudes. This exclusion from technology tends to influence the career aspirations of girls and to limit their options in vocational training.

In recent years, some countries have introduced changes in this gender-based curriculum differentiation to address the problems of inequality in access to skills. In the early 1980s, Malaysia introduced a compulsory programme in life skills and Sri Lanka experimented with a compulsory life-skills programme to ensure a common core of practical skills for boys and girls. More recently, Japan, the Republic of Korea and the Philippines have endeavoured to equip both girls and boys with knowledge and skills in technology and home economics in the general education curriculum.

There has been no clear gender focus in policy in the vocational training subsector, however, although both the National Policy on Education in India (1986) and the Philippine Plan for Gender Responsive Development (1995–2025), referred to increasing the access of women to a wide range of technical and vocational skills. Consequently there are wide gender disparities in enrolment in vocational training programmes in all countries, both in those with a broad base of general education and in those with a narrow base. In Sri Lanka, 70 percent of women seeking entry to technical colleges opt for commerce, secretarial, and home economics courses and women are under-represented in technical courses. Around 90 percent of women trainees in vocational centres organized by the Ministries of Labour and Vocational Training, and Education, and the majority of those in the programmes of the National Apprenticeship and Industrial Training Authority and National Youth Services Council, are enrolled in sewing and dressmaking courses. Agricultural training courses tend to domesticate women and training programmes in the construction industry are apt to bypass them (Jayaweera 1995a). In Pakistan's gender-segregated institutions, 52 percent of secondary-level vocational institutions are for women exclusively, but women trainees are only 30 percent of the total vocational enrolment (Chowdhury 1996). In India, 15 percent of the enrolment in second-level technical and vocational courses, and 0.3 percent of those in engineering trades, are women (Nayar 1993). Thirty-five percent of the enrolment in technical schools in Malaysia were women in 1990, and 50 percent of these women were technical trainees (Sidin 1996). Bangladesh has one women's polytechnic and a quota of 15 percent is enforced in other institutions, and in Nepal's agrarian society, a quota of 10 to 20 percent women has been introduced in agricultural institutes in the current five-year plan. A recent project in the Philippines to train women in non-traditional trades (WINT) and a new project in Sri Lanka to increase the access of young women to vocational information, particularly on non-traditional areas, and to change attitudes, are major efforts in reducing inequality in access to skills required by changes in economies.

These gender imbalances are reflected also in faculty- or course-based enrolment data in universities. In more traditional societies such as Bangladesh, Nepal and India, gender gaps are wide, but in more liberal societies, such as Sri Lanka and Malaysia, imbalances have been reduced except in technology (see table 2). In the Philippines women constitute 63 to 73 percent of the enrolment in higher education institutions and are half or more of the students in all courses except in engineering (14.1 percent) (NCRW 1995). The distribution of skills is even less equitable in the most industrialized country, Japan (see table 2). Disparities are wider in countries in which "gender screening" has taken place.

Table 2. Gender Imbalances in Enrolment in University Courses (Percentages)

Courses	Bangladesh	Nepal	India	Sri Lanka	Malaysia	Japan
Medicine	27	49.3	31.7	42.9	51.8	
Dentistry				52.1		
Vet. Science			5.8	44.1		
Agriculture	7	0.6	4.9	44.6		
Engineering	6	5.5		12.2	14.5	11
Eng. & Tech.			6.2			
Architecture				47.4		
Science			32.6	41.4	56.0	9
Health Sc.		5.4				21
Management		14.0		44.1		
Law		5.0	8.7	56.9		
Commerce						
& Business			20.5		42.3	
Soc. Science				55.9	53.2	11
Education			43.2			7
Humanities		37.0	52.4			41
College						
Courses	37					
Gen. Univ.						
Courses	20					

Sources: Bangladesh — Jabbar 1992; Nepal — UNESCO, 1990; India — Indiresan, 1995; Sir Lanka — Jayaweera, 1995; Malaysia — Ariffin, 1992; Japan — NEWC, 1990
Some sources give only rounded numbers.

It is apparent that social norms underpinning gender tracking in schools, and progressively in vocational training programmes and higher education institutions, create a continuum of gender inequality that conflicts with the basic principle of equal educational opportunity to which all countries are committed, even as a distant goal. There appears, however, to be no such awareness or commitment to promote gender equality in the outcomes of education goals or policies in terms such as knowledge, skills and traits that affect the life chances of women and their well-being in their multiple roles. A critical example is the narrow range of skills acquired, perforce, by women and the consequent inadequacies in female labour supply in countries, many of which are in the process of economic transformation.

Education and the labour market

Although public perceptions of a positive link between education and employment have prevailed since the establishment of modern education institutions, the efficacy of education as an agent of gender equality in the world of work has been seen to be limited by the inequitable distribution of employment-related skills and traits among women and men. The interface between class and the social construction of gender also distort the demand for female labour. Consequently, there does not appear to be a positive linear relationship between education and women's occupational mobility and economic rewards relative to the position of men in the employment structure. It was seen that women have equal access with men to elementary education in around fifteen countries in Asia. Women in fewer countries have equal access to secondary and higher education, which are perceived to be the avenues to relatively satisfactory incomes and upward mobility, and there are no countries in which women have equal access to vocational training. It is a moot point whether all women have equal access with men to employment commensurate with their educational levels.

Labour-force participation rates are unlikely to be reliable indicators of gender equality in employment, since women — who have been traditionally economic producers in subsistence agriculture and home-based industries in these countries for centuries — are unrecognized and not counted in modern labour-force computations. Nevertheless, even this underestimated female labour force has been increasing faster than the male labour force since the 1960s. In the earlier phase in many countries, access to secondary and higher education brought women from their homes to professional and semi-professional jobs and raised their status in society. Since the late 1960s, however, female labour force participation rates have risen at all levels of educational attainment, in response largely to economic pressures on families. Hence, education per se has not accelerated access to employment for many women. The experience in Asia has shown that two variables, labour market structures and gender-related norms and stereotypes, affect the operation of education as an instrument of gender equality in the labour market.

Many women have been faced with the rising incidence of unemployment, chiefly female unemployment in countries in which slow economic growth limited the capacity of the economy to absorb the expanding labour force, including increasing output of the education system. This situation obtained in low-enrolment countries such as Bangladesh (Islam 1994), and India (Ghosh and Talbani 1996) and more particularly in countries in which educational expansion outran economic growth, such as the Philippines (NCRFW 1985), Sri Lanka (Alailima 1992), and Indonesia (Oey-Gardiner and Riga-Adiwoso 1996).

An extreme example is that of Sri Lanka, where the unemployment rate of women has been double that of the unemployment rate of men consistently since the end of the 1960s. The most vulnerable groups have been secondary school leavers and university arts graduates, and the unemployment rates of women school leavers and university arts graduates have been significantly higher than those of their male counterparts. All those who enter the labour market are found to have difficulties in getting jobs, irrespective of their education level. Unlike three decades ago, women with secondary school and higher education attainment join a large labour reserve. The interface of social class and gender compounds difficulties as it is largely upper and middle-class women with secondary or higher educational attainment who achieve rapid occupational mobility through education (Jayaweera 1995b). Even in an affluent country such as Japan, structural unemployment limited the employment prospects of women junior college and university graduates in the 1980s (NWEC 1990). More recently, women who have been concentrated in the public sector over the years, have been "involuntarily retired" in countries in which IMF-World Bank structural adjustment programmes reduce the public sector in employment (Commonwealth Secretariat 1990).

Despite rising educational levels in many countries, globalization, deregulation in the labour market, and the liberalization of economies, and other macroeconomic policies, have incorporated women in the global market on unequal terms. In the 1980s, the percentage of women in professional and semi-professional employment in countries in which women were well represented in secondary and higher education, was relatively high: 62 percent in the Philippines, 49.5 percent in Sri Lanka, 43.1 percent in Malaysia and 42.6 percent in Japan. But underemployment of women graduates in middle-level secretarial employment has become a common practice in all countries, including Japan, and significantly, since the 1980s the incremental female labour force has been thrust into marginal economic activities to meet a demand for female labour that virtually devalues education as an agent of advancement.

The international division of labour established by the relocation of labour-intensive industries by transnational corporations in economically developing countries created a demand for low-cost female labour as easily dispensable secondary earners. This "comparative advantage" stimulated states to organize "Export Processing Zones" with a preponderance of young women workers, in East Asia in the 1950s and 1960s, Southeast Asia in the 1960s and 1970s, and South Asia in the 1980s and 1990s. Around 80 percent of the labour force — in chiefly garment and electronic enterprises within and outside the zones and in subcontracting industries — have been women employed in fragmented, semi-skilled jobs with few prospects for upgrading their skills and achieving occupational mobility, while men have been employed chiefly as managers and technicians in these factories (Heyzer 1988). Industrialization in Asia has depended heavily on the cheap labour of women.

The demand in the international labour market for domestic women workers in oil-rich countries in West Asia, economically prosperous countries in the Middle East and in Southeast Asia and even in countries in Western Europe, led to an influx of "housemaids" from low-income countries in Asia such as the Philippines, Sri Lanka, Thailand, and Bangladesh to these countries. These women workers are often unprotected by labour contracts and, while making a significant contribution to the revenue of their countries, have had no opportunities of improving their own employment prospects, while overseas men workers are employed chiefly as skilled or technical workers. Women university graduates in the Philippines are compelled, in the face of unemployment, to seek overseas employment as domestic workers, or in another vulnerable occupation, as entertainers in the hospitality trade (Heyzer 1994).

In the informal sector, women have been thrust into the position of unpaid family workers as a result of the rising costs of production in the agricultural sector associated with the reduction in producer subsidies under structural adjustment programmes. Although self-employment has been perceived by national policymakers as a panacea for employment, women have been apt to be perceived as secondary earners, rather than as potential entrepreneurs. They have access to credit and have been mobilized for group activities, but lack of skills and technology has reinforced their low productivity and low-income syndrome and has perpetuated their poverty status.

The pattern of demand for female labour in changing economies has consequently widened gender inequalities in the labour market in all countries, notwithstanding the reduction in the gender gap in general education in most countries. Gender-role stereotypes are not only imbedded in these demand factors, but gendered social norms and assumptions also exacerbate constraints to gender equality.

In conservative societies such as Bangladesh, India, Pakistan and Nepal, women, even women graduates, have been denied the opportunity to enter the labour market by social disapproval of paid employment outside the home, and its reflection on the prestige of the husband in the context of the ideology of male breadwinner and home-based housewife. Women in low-income families have been compelled by economic pressures to seek employment despite this normative prescription, but to many women in better-off families, education has been a personal fulfilment and not an avenue to economic equality (Chanana 1988; Huq 1992; Acharya 1994).

In affluent Japan, women's reproductive role is perceived to take precedence over economic activities, irrespective of educational qualifications. Japanese women, particularly women graduates, tend to remain at home in a supportive role to husbands who rise steadily in the employment hierarchy, or they quit work after marriage or childbirth. Some of them return to employment after their children are grown up, and either opt for or are marginalized in part-time employment (Matsui 1996). It appears that access to education has failed to change the secondary status of many Japanese women as supplementary income earners or supportive wives.

In Asia, education has not changed significantly the traditional gender-based segregation in the labour market. Women in all countries continue to be concentrated in the agricultural sector as family workers, or in traditional and assembly-line industries, and in chiefly education, health, and domestic services in the service sector, and are under-represented in technical and managerial employment. Gender-based discrimination by employers has reinforced asymmetry in employment. In both Japan and China, companies are reported to overtly prefer to employ men, despite the provisions in Japan of the Equal Employment

Opportunity Act introduced in 1986. In Sri Lanka, around half the graduates from agriculture faculties in universities have been employed as teachers and not as professionals in the agriculture sector (CENWOR 1992). Women engineers complained of discrimination, of jobs reserved for men, and of male preference at recruitment and in promotion (Jayaweera and Sanmugam 1992).

The strongest barrier to gender equality in employment is the "glass ceiling" that prevents qualified women from reaching the highest management positions in the public and private sectors on equal terms with men. Although several women have emerged through the democratic process of election at the highest level of political leadership as presidents and prime ministers in South Asia and in the Philippines, education has not contributed to this development. It is interesting to note also from a gender perspective, that in countries in which around half or more of students in higher education institutions and members of some professions are women, less than 20 percent have reached senior-level positions and only a microscopic minority are visible at the highest decision-making level. In Bangladesh, 10 percent of Class 1 administrators are women because a quota has been imposed for recruitment. But no women are secretaries to ministries, heads of district administrations, managing directors of private enterprises, vice-chancellors of universities, and even the top positions in the Ministry of Women's Affairs and posts of heads of some women's colleges are held by men (Islam 1996). The situation is not very different in Japan, where women are in less than 5 percent of the high-level positions in administration, the judiciary, and foreign services; less than 1 percent in private companies; and around 5 percent of professors in universities and around 25 percent in the "feminine" environment of junior colleges (NWEC 1990).

In the Philippines, a country with relatively equal access to educational opportunity, 63 percent of higher education students and 66 percent of the senior academic staff are women, but 60 percent of administrators are men. Half the second-level positions in the Civil Service in the Philippines are held by women but only around 1 percent are at the highest level (NCRFW 1995). In Sri Lanka, 16.1 percent of the Class 1 Administrative Service and 12.2 percent of deans in universities are women, but there is only one woman Cabinet Secretary, and no vice-chancellors, or high-level managers in private enterprises. It is only in the Philippines and India that women function as vice-chancellors, and in India also, as chairperson of the University Grants Commission.

In production and services in which large numbers of women are concentrated, education levels have become increasingly irrelevant as criteria in the demand for female labour. There have been, consequently, reversals in occupational mobility in recent years in countries such as the Philippines and Sri Lanka, in which educational expansions took place over three decades ago. For all women, inequalities are rooted in socially constructed perceptions of the reproductive role of women as an impediment to economic productivity, and myths and assumptions of gender appropriate jobs that identify technology and management as domains in which women have low "innate" capabilities. Women have responded to labour-market demand for family survival, maintenance, and mobility, but have tended often to internalise gendered norms and to hesitate to accept the challenge of positions of authority and rapid technological change.

Women with the same educational attainment but from different socioeconomic backgrounds have unequal opportunities. Women and men with the same educational attainment are likely to reach unequal positions. Such bifurcation in the route from education to employment is consonant with the vertical and horizontal segmentation of the labour market.

Gender relations within the family

In the context of the patriarchal values that underpin the social relations of production and family relations, and dichotomous perceptions of the status of a "mother" and "women," education has a potentially powerful role in promoting gender equality in the family. It can ensure an equitable distribution of knowledge and skills that will enhance the status of women in the family and expand their economic roles, particularly outside the household. As an agent of socialisation it can promote perceptions of equitable gender roles and work sharing among women and men, and improve the self-perceptions and self-confidence of women to enable them to safeguard their fundamental rights. Whether education performs these functions effectively in at least some segments of societies is not clear from the conflicting evidence that surfaces from microstudies (CENWOR 1989; Ilo 1990; Acharya 1994). It is possible, however, to examine the relative contribution that education has made to promoting a more equitable division of labour and an equal share in decision making within the family, and providing more space for women's autonomy.

There is a consensus in all countries that there has not been a radical change in the gender division of labour. In East, Southeast, and South Asia, the ideology of child-care responsibilities and household chores as "women's work" prevails and has been internalized by generations of women. It has been estimated consequently that, on average, women work a minimum of fourteen hours a day to carry out their multiple roles, while men work around nine hours. Increasing female labour-force participation has not changed the gender division of labour within and outside the household. In more egalitarian communities, dual-earner families that are partly the outcome of educational aspirations and economic pressures have moved towards a more equitable sharing of household tasks. Instances of role reversal caused by the adoption of the role of primary income earner by women or by overseas migration of women for employment, have been noted in these countries. Education, however, has yet to change perceptions of gender roles and their implications for gender relations significantly in all societies.

Decision making patterns vary from male dominance to joint decision making by spouses. Education increases women's credibility as decision makers, but there is strong evidence that the critical factors that ensure gender equality in decision making are economic participation, more often outside the household, substantial contribution to family income, access to an independent income, and economic independence in controlling the income generated, regardless of educational attainments. Wage earners and salaried women who have control of their own income have a greater say in decision making than women with the same educational attainment who do not seek employment, or are not permitted to seek employment, or whose income is subsumed as family income over which they have no control. Sharing in decision making ensures, in turn, more equitable allocation of resources within the family such as access to education.

The aspect of gender relations to which education has yet to make a significant contribution is the control of female behaviour through puberty and marriage rituals, control of female sexuality, and gender-based violence within the family. Women at all educational levels acquiesce in or are victims of dowry bargaining, virginity tests, female circumcision and domestic violence, and in India, in dowry deaths and female foeticide and infanticide. Education has delayed marriage and reduced family size, and contraceptive use is increasingly prevalent, but women yet face male dominance or state authority in control of their own fertility.

Education to the highest level can promote economic independence, and consequently gender equality in the family. Education can be used positively as an agent of socializing girls and boys, women and men, for equality. Yet even educated women tend to socialize their sons and daughters to reproduce gender inequality within the family and in society.

Conclusion

Notwithstanding the claim in the United Nations Human Development Report (UNDP 1995) that the gender gap has been reduced in education, progress has been seen to be slow in the 1980s and 1990s in Asia. Gender disparities in enrolment continue to be very wide in Nepal and Pakistan in primary education, in many countries in secondary and higher education, and in all countries in vocational education. Equal access to education in some countries is still the privilege of the elite. This Asian experience supports the view expressed in the report that equal access to education, or even access of a segment of the population to education, has not ensured gender equality in the outcomes of education in terms of economically rewarding employment and access to decision making positions in the public sphere, or, it needs to be added, in gender relations in the family. The interface of class and gender and their impact on macroeducational, -social and -economic policies have created structural constraints to equality in the education system and in the labour market. Family relationships have continued to restrict women's autonomy and to be the most resistant to change.

Education has contributed visibly to expanding the horizons of generations of women and to improving their status in society and their physical quality of life. Education, per se, has not been able to compensate for macroeconomic constraints and poverty of family resources or to counter the social construction of gender that underpins gender inequality in all institutions and social practices. In the past, education policies were sometimes confined to rhetorical statements and were abortive in action. Ingredients of success have been political commitment, adequate incentives beyond basic needs, and equitable distribution of facilities. Education policies did not, however, seek to transform gendered attitudes, behavioural expectations, and ideologies which are embedded in macroeconomic policies, labour-market structures, and family relationships, and are important overt and hidden determinants of outcomes of policies.

References

Acharya, Meena. 1994. *The Statistical Profile on Nepalese Women*. Kathmandu: Institute for Integrated Development Studies.
Alailima, Patricia. 1992. 'Education-Employment Linkages: The Macro-Profile' in *Sri Lanka Journal of Social Sciences* 15(1 & 2): 1–46.
Ariffin, Jamilah. 1992. *Women and Development in Malaysia*. Malaysia: Pelenduk.

Bisaria, Sarojini. 1985. *Identification and Elimination of Sex Stereotypes in and from Education Programmes and school textbooks.* Paris: UNESCO.

Bourdieu, P., and J. Passeron. 1977. *Reproduction in Education and Society,* London: Sage.

Centre for Women's Research (CENWOR). 1989. *Women's Work and Family Strategies.* Colombo: Centre for Women's Research.

CENWOR. 1992. *Women Graduates in Agriculture.* Study Series, no.3. Colombo, Sri Lanka: Centre for Women's Research.

Chanana, Karuna. 1988. *Socialisation, Education and Women.* New Dehli: Orient Longmans.

Chowdhury, Kowsar P. 1996. Pakistan. In Grace C.L. Mak, ed., *Women, Education and Development in Asia.* 187–216. New York and London: Garland Publishing.

Commonwealth Secretariat. 1990. *Engendering Adjustment for the 1990s.* London: Malborough House.

Ghosh, Ratna, and Abdulaziz Talbani. 1996. India. In Grace, C.L. Mak, ed., *Women, Education and Development in Asia.* 165-186. New York and London: Garland Publishing.

Halsey, A.H., A.C. Heath, and J. M. Ridge. 1980. *Origins and Destinations. Family, Class and Education in Modern Britain.* Oxford: Clarendon Press.

Hassan, Iftikhar. 1982. *The Psychological Profile of Rural Women.* Islamabad, Pakistan: National Institute of Psychology.

Heyzer, Noeleen, ed. 1988. *Daughters in Industry.* Kuala Lumpur: Asia and Pacific Development Centre.

Heyzer, Noeleen, ed. 1994. *The Trade in Domestic Workers: Causes, Mechanisms and Consequences of International Migration.* Kuala Lumpur: Asia and Pacific Development Centre; and UK: Zed Books.

Huq, Jahanara. 1992. Women in secondary and higher education: Myth and realities. In *Education and Gender Equity: Bangladesh.* 41–53. Dhaka: Women for Women.

Ilo, Jeanne. 1990. *Fishers, Traders, Farmers, Wives.* Philippines: Institute of Philippine Culture, Ateneo de Manila University.

Indiresan, J. 1995. *Moving Beyond Access: Gender Positive Initiatives in Women's Colleges.* New Delhi: National Institute of Educational Planning and Administration.

Islam, Mahmuda. 1994. *Whither Women's Studies in Bangladesh.* Dhaka, Bangladesh: Women for Women.

Islam, Mahmuda. 1996. *Women Managers in Higher Education in Bangladesh.* Colombo, Sri Lanka: Commonwealth Regional Workshop on Women and Management in Higher Education. Jan.1997.

Islam, Shamima. 1982. *Women's Education in Bangladesh.* Dhaka, Bangladesh: The Foundation for Research on Educational Planning and Development.

170 Gender Issues in International Education:Beyond Policy

Jabbar, M.A. 1992. Historical role of women: Social change in education. In *Education and Gender Equity in Bangladesh*. Dhaka: Women for Women.

Jarillas, Myrna I. and Socorro M. Diaz. 1994. *Women and Education in the Philippines*. Paper. Bangkok: ESCAP.

Jayaweera, Swarna. 1993. The Socialization of the girl child. In *Shadows and Vistas*, 148–82. Colombo, Sri Lanka: Centre for Women's Research

Jayaweera, Swarna. 1995a. Women and education. In *Facets of Change*, 96–130. Colombo, Sri Lanka: Centre for Women's Research.

Jayaweera, Swarna. 1995b. Women, education and occupational mobility. In *Facing Odds: Women in the Labour Market*, 148–63. Colombo, Sri Lanka: Centre for Women's Research.

Jayaweera, Swarna. 1996. Sri Lanka. In Grace C.L. Mak, ed., *Women, Education and Development in Asia*. New York and London: Garland Publishing.

Jayaweera, Swarna, and Thana Sanmugam, 1992. *Women Engineers in Sri Lanka*. Colombo: Sri Lanka Federation of University Women.

Khan, Salma. 1992. Education policy, programme and women: A road to gender equity. In *Education and Gender Equity: Bangladesh*, 87–97. Dhaka: Women for Women.

Korean Women's Development Institute (KWDI). 1985. *A Study on Gender Roles in Primary School Textbooks*. Seoul: KWDI.

KWDI. 1986. *A Study on Gender Roles in the Secondary School Curricula*. Seoul: KWDI.

Mak, Grace. C.L. 1996. The People's Republic of China. In Grace C.L. Mak, ed., *Women, Education and Development in Asia*, 3–28. New York and London: Garland Publishing.

Matsui, Machiko. 1996. Japan. In Grace C.L. Mak, ed., *Women, Education and Development in Asia*, 29–50. New York and London: Garland Publishing.

Mazumdar, Vina. 1988. *Gender Issues and Educational Development*, An Occasional Paper, No.15. New Delhi: Centre for Women's Development Studies.

Ministry of Human Resources Development (MHRD). 1986. *National Policy on Education*. New Delhi: Department of Education.

Ministry of Human Resources Development (MHRD). 1992. *Plan of Action on Education*. New Delhi: Department of Education.

Ministry of Women's Affairs. 1993. *Women's Charter (Sri Lanka)*. Colombo, Sri Lanka.

Ministry of Women's Affairs. 1996. *National Plan for Action: Towards Gender Equality*. Colombo, Sri Lanka.

National Committee on the Role of Filipino Women (NCRFW). 1985. *The Women's Decade in the Philippines*. Manila.

NCRFW. 1995. *Philippine Plan for Gender Responsive Development*. Manila.

National Women's Education Centre (NWEC). 1990. *Women in a Changing Society: the Japanese Scene*. Tokyo: NWEC and UNESCO.

Nayar, Usha. 1993. *Girls' and Women's Education in India*. New Delhi: NCERT, Department of Women's Studies.

Oey-Gardiner, Mayling, and Suprapto Riga-Adiwoso. 1996. Indonesia. In Grace C.L. Mak, ed., *Women, Education and Development in Asia*, 95–118. New York and London: Garland Publishing.

Schultz, T.W. 1963. *The Economic Value of Education*. New York: Columbia University Press.

Shamim, Ishrat. 1995. *Towards Beijing and Beyond: Women Shaping Policies in Areas of Concern*. Dhaka, Bangladesh: PACT. Centre for Women and Children's Studies.

Sidin, Robiah. 1996. Malaysia. In Grace C.L. Mak, ed., *Women, Education and Development in Asia*, 9119–43. New York and London: Garland Publishing.

United Nations Development Programme (UNDP). 1995. *Human Development Report, 1995*. New York: United Nations.

UNESCO. 1990. *Women's Participation in Higher Education: China, Nepal and the Philippines*. Bangkok: UNESCO.

Contributors

Sally Brown is Deputy Principal and Professor of Education at the University of Stirling, Scotland. She was formerly the Director of the Scottish Council for Research in Education. Her current research interests focus on matters of equal opportunities, especially gender and disability issues, and teachers' thinking about teaching and learning. She has been working in educational research for more than a quarter of a century, and has more than one hundred publications. Before that she taught physics at high school and university levels.

Rebecca Priegert Coulter is Associate Dean of the Faculty of Education, University of Western Ontario. Her research interests lie in the areas of the history of youth and gender and schooling. Her current work explores women's organizing in education and the gender dimensions of educational restructuring in Canada. Recent articles appear in the *Canadian Journal of Education, Gender and Education* and *Canadian Women's Studies*, and as chapters in several edited collections.

Hetty Dekkers is a member of the management team of the Institute for Applied Social Studies of Nijmegen University, where she co-ordinates educational research, particularly on the school careers of disadvantaged groups and school effectiveness in this area. The special focus of this research concerns girls and children from ethnic minority groups and low-income families. Her other research interests include policy towards such groups and early school-leaving. Her publications include work undertaken for the Dutch government on equal opportunities policies in education.

Sheena Erskine currently devotes her time and energy to educational research in the area of special educational needs and equal opportunities in education. She has worked in Scotland as a teacher and headteacher, and spent some years working as an administrator. Her publications include work in the area of the professionalism of teachers and gender issues in education. She has made contributions on this topic at the World Congress of Comparative Education Societies.

Karin Hyde is an education consultant based in Nairobi. She focuses on issues of access, achievement, and dropout among young girls. This chapter was written while she was a research fellow at the Centre for Social Research, University of Malawi, and is based on research funded by the Rockefeller Foundation.

Swarna Jayaweera is Emeritus Professor of Education, University of Colombo. She has a Master's and a Doctorate degree of the Institute of Education, University of London and was postdoctoral Fellow at Columbia University, New York. She has taught in the Universities of Perideniya and Colombo and she was also UNESCO Adviser and UNICEF Consultant on the Access of Women to Education in Nepal and has been a consultant to UN agencies and bilateral agencies in Sri Lanka and in the Asian Region. She is one of the founders of the Centre for Women's Research (CENWOR) and is its Joint Co-ordinator. She has contributed extensively to books and to international and local journals on women and on education. She is presently a member of the National Committee for Women and is a Research Fellow of the Faculty of Graduate Studies of the University of Colombo.

Jane Kenway is Director of the Deakin Centre for Education and Change. She is an Associate Professor in the Faculty of Education at Deakin University in Victoria, Australia, and teaches in the postgraduate administration programme. She has published widely on policy issues in education. Her work includes *Marketing and Education: Some Critical Issues* (Deakin University Press, 1995); J. Kenway and Willis (1995), *Critical Visions: Rewriting the Future of Gender, Education and Work* (Canberra: Australian Government Publishing Service); J. Blackmore and J. Kenway, eds., *Gender Matters in Educational Administration and Policy: A Feminist Introduction* (London: Falmer Press, 1993) and *Answering Back: Teachers, Students and Feminism in Schools* (London: Allen & Unwin, 1996).

Sheila Riddell has recently taken up the post of Professor of Social Policy (Disability Studies) at Glasgow University. Following her PhD on *Gender and Option Choice in Two Rural Comprehensive Schools*, at Bristol University in 1988, she worked as Research Fellow in the Department of Education, University of Edinburgh, on a project investigating the impact of the 1981 Education (Scotland) Act, on children with special educational needs. From 1989 to 1996 she taught and researched at Stirling University and was promoted to a Personal

Chair in 1995, followed by a period as Dean of Arts and Social Science at Napier University, Edinburgh. She has researched and written extensively in the areas of special educational needs/disability and gender and education.

Nelly P. Stromquist is Professor of Education at the University of Southern California in Los Angeles, specializing in international development education, which she observes from a sociological perspective. Her research addresses questions of gender, equity policy, and adult education in developing countries, particularly Latin America and West Africa. Her most recent work includes authoring the book *Literacy for Citizenship: Gender and Grassroots Dynamics in Brazil* (New York: Suny Press, 1997), and editing *Gender Dimensions in Education in Latin America* (OAS, 1996) and *The Encyclopedia of Third World Women* (New York: Garland Publishing, forthcoming).

Margaret B. Sutherland is Professor Emeritus of Education, University of Leeds. Her main interests are comparative education and the education of girls and women: she has researched and published widely in these fields. She is the immediate past president of AFEC (Association Francophone d'Education Comparée), an Honorary Fellow of the Scottish Council for Research in Education, an Honorary Member of CESE (Comparative Education Society in Europe), and has served as chair and co-chair of the Gender Issues Commission of various World Congresses of Comparative Education.

Karen Tregenza is a Research Fellow in the Faculty of Education, Deakin University, Geelong. She has been involved in a broad range of research projects spanning many educational issues in areas including vocational education, youth, marketisation of schools, health and physical education and the use of new technologies.

Eileen Turner is a researcher at the University of Stirling. She has worked on many projects concerned with assessment, staff development, and school links with business and arts organisations. Recently completed projects include: *Gender Equality in Scottish Schools: The Impact of Recent Educational Reforms*, with Sally Brown and Sheila Riddell, which was funded by the Equal Opportunities Commission and *Women in Further Education Management : Roles, Routes and Perceptions*, a joint project with the Scottish Further Education Unit funded by the Scottish Office Education and Industry Department. Current research includes *"The Arts-Education Interface:*

Evaluating Quality" and *"Under-Achievement in the First Years of Secondary Education."*

Peter Watkins is a senior lecturer in the Faculty of Education, Geelong. He has had a long interest in vocational education, being involved with the work-experience program at Bentleigh High in the 1970s. He completed a PhD on school and work in 1981 before joining Deakin University in the MEd Administration area. He has had numerous monographs and papers on work and education published, many appearing in such international journals as *British Journal of Sociology of Education, Journal of Policy Studies, Australian Journal of Education, Discourse.*

Maggie Wilson is a principal lecturer at Oxford Brookes University, with a remit for developing international award-bearing work in the field of educational studies. She has a particular research interest in education and in comparative education. Among her publications are *Girls and Young Women in Education: A European Perspective* (Oxford: Pergamon Press) and *Women in Educational Management: A European Perspective* (London: Paul Chapman Publishing).

Index

For Product Safety Concerns and Information please contact our EU
representative GPSR@taylorandfrancis.com
Taylor & Francis Verlag GmbH, Kaufingerstraße 24, 80331 München, Germany

www.ingramcontent.com/pod-product-compliance
Lightning Source LLC
Chambersburg PA
CBHW050711280326
41926CB00088B/2926